RetireSmart II

The Gig Economy Edition

Mark Anthony Grimaldi

First Edition

PAGE PUBLISHING
Conneaut Lake, PA

First originally published by Page Publishing 2022

ISBN 978-1-6624-7614-3 (pbk)
ISBN 978-1-6624-7617-4 (hc)
ISBN 978-1-6624-7616-7 (digital)

Printed in the United States of America

To my father who lost his sight when I was a young boy
but never lost his vision for the man I would become.

Contents

Acknowledgments

This book would not be possible without the guidance of the very talented Mr. Frank J. Fabio, CPA and Ms. Julie Schaeffer.

Introduction

In the following pages, I will show you how to save for retirement as a participant in the "gig" economy.

My plan is built on how to create tax-free retirement income. I will explain how to

- create your gig retirement account *tax free*,
- withdraw from your gig retirement account income *tax free*, and
- pass the balance to your loved ones *tax free*.

That's it. Interested?

How is this possible, you ask? Actually, it's simple. All you need to do is apply three basic tax codes the proper way. Are these "loopholes" only available to the rich? Nope. They are accessible to everyone and are hiding in plain sight. In fact, I bet you've used one, if not two, doing your most recent tax filing. The problem is you may not have used them properly. Warren Buffet does. Jeff Bezos does. Your rich uncle and aunt do. Now you will too.

Buckle your seatbelt because you're about to be shown the secrets that the rich have used for decades. You may be thinking, *I'm not a financial whiz, I hope this is easy to follow.* I promise you it's very simple. In fact, it's so simple you are going to think, *That's it? That's all I need to do?* Yes, that's it. But first, I need to let you in on the secret.

Image a retirement plan that offers the following. Well, it exists, and I call it the "RetireSmart *gig* retirement account."

- Has no contribution limits
- Has no investment choice limitations

- Lets you touch your money when you need it most
- Knows the tax difference between income and capital gains
- Has no age restrictions on your money
- Has no distribution minimums
- Understands the tax code
- Has no 10 percent excise taxes on distributions
- Has no 1099Rs
- Has no administration expenses
- Can be funded from any source
- Has no CPA expenses
- Has no vesting requirements

Does that sound too good to be true? Again, I promise you it isn't. Every claim I made is true and has been for decades—period. All I ask is that you forget everything you've been told about retirement plans and start anew today.

In my first book, *The Money Compass*, the chapter about 401(k) plans got the most attention. My readers couldn't believe their 401(k) plans benefited no one but Uncle Sam. And that made me want to write a book dedicated to explaining one of the biggest financial misdirections in history: the 401(k) plan.

In my last seven-time-award-winning book, *RetireSmart*, my mission, and I hope I was successful, was to show you how to build a secure retirement plan without using a 401(k). Why is this so important to "gig" workers? Because very few of you are eligible for a 401(k).

It's something I've thought about a lot as a practicing economist for more than thirty years. I feel it on a visceral level almost every day because I see people who have clearly done so poorly. When I walk into retail- and food-service establishments, for example, I often see older folks working physically demanding jobs for a near-minimum wage. Some may be trying to stay busy; others may want to cover some fun extras in their life. But are many working those jobs because they need to or because they didn't save wisely for retirement, or is it something different entirely? I would like to suggest it was how they thought about retirement savings, or more directly, it's how they were programmed to think about saving for retirement. I think that we are all being told a huge lie about saving for retirement, more specifically that 401(k)s and IRAs are our only options. This is simply not true.

But let's begin our current journey by talking about the millions of hard-working Americans who make up the gig economy—those individuals who wake up every day (or night or whenever their iPhone notifies them) and go to work.

That's you. Let's talk about you.

Part 1

Understanding the Gig Economy

Chapter 1

What is the Gig Economy?

The gig economy is empowerment. This new business paradigm empowers individuals to better shape their own destiny and leverage their existing assets to their benefit.

—John McAfee

The gig economy—also known as the sharing economy or on-demand economy—is a free-market system of temporary employment.

You may think of gig workers as freelancers or independent contractors or even part-time hires, but however you categorize them, they're increasing in number and changing the way the world looks at work.

That change will not be linear. As I write this, we are in the midst of a pandemic. While we're learning more and more about the SARS-CoV-2 virus every day—and managing it more effectively—life has not yet returned to normal, and the road ahead is long. The emergence of the virus has changed the gig economy; the defeat of the virus will likely do the same.

But I can say with certainty that some things will not change. One of the main drivers of the gig economy—technology—is here to stay. All in, the stage is set for the gig economy to see sustained growth, perhaps even explosive growth. It's just a matter of where and how we experience that growth.

Origin and rise of the gig economy

The term "gig" is slang for a temporary job. Typically used by musicians, it dates back to the early 1900s when jazz musicians coined the term to refer to their performances.

But the term stuck and with it, came a job market—the rise of temporary work following the Great Depression. By 1995, 10 percent of Americans had "alternative" work arrangements, by which I mean they considered themselves freelancers, intendant contractors, temporary agents, or on-call workers.

Then as we entered the digital era, the gig economy exploded. In 1996, Craig Newmark started Craigslist, which eventually included job listings. In 2005, Amazon began hiring gig workers to perform so-called "microtasks" deemed too complex for artificial intelligence, such as transcription. And in 2008, TaskRabbit was launched to hire individuals to complete simple chores. Then came Airbnb (designed by roommates in an attempt to make rent) and Uber. Since 2009, however, the use of the word "gig" has expanded to refer to all sorts of freelance work, making it a *Merriam-Webster* word to watch.

Technology is likely the biggest enabler of the gig economy. Digitization has created more jobs that can be done from afar, and with a laptop and Wi-Fi, workers can do their jobs from just about anywhere—including overseas, where the cost of labor is significantly lower than it is in the United States and other developed nations. As a result, jobs and locations are being decoupled. Freelancers can offer their assistance on projects originating around the world, and employers can select the best individuals from a larger pool than is available in any given locale.

The Global Financial Crisis also likely enabled the gig economy. It is notable that gig work grew significantly around 2008 and 2009 when struggling companies turned to freelancers as a means of managing their fixed costs amid economic uncertainty.

The entrance of the millennial generation (and Generation Z, the demographic cohort succeeding millennials) into the labor market has further driven this trend. The first generation to grow up in the era of everywhere internet, millennials are technologically advanced and highly connected. According to a 2019 analysis by Pew Research Center, 93 percent own smartphones compared with 90 percent of Generation X, 68 percent of baby boomers, and 40 percent of the silent generation. This makes millennials perfectly suited for a world in which work can increasingly be done remotely via digital platforms and the workforce is becoming increasingly mobile. Generation Z is even more in tune with mobile work. It's a symbiotic relationship.

Today, the gig economy is part of a shifting cultural and business environment that also includes the sharing economy (with ride-sharing and food delivery, for example) and the barter economy (trading goods for goods).

Size of the gig economy

Roughly fifty-seven million people or around 35 percent of the US workforce are freelancers, according to two sources: Gallup's 2018 "Gig Economy and Alternative Work Arrangements" study and a 2019 report from Upwork (a popular online platform that connected freelancers with companies seeking them) and Freelancers Union, "Freelancing in America: 2019."

These gig workers contribute nearly $1trillion in freelancing income to the economy or nearly 5 percent of US gross domestic product (GDP), according to Upwork and Freelancers Union.

But these numbers are expected to grow. As Fabio Rosati, CEO of Upwork stated, "This is just the start: The connected era we live in is liberating our workforce. The barriers to being a freelance professional—finding work, collaborating with clients, and getting paid on time—are going away."

Most popular gigs

A variety of industries utilizes gigs. The most obvious are creative fields: media and communications, including art, photography, graphic design, and writing. But other professional fields also employ gig workers. Information technology (including software development, security engineering, and network analysis), finance (including bookkeeping and mortgage representatives), and education (substitute instructors and tutors) are notable examples. Other common gigs include construction (carpenters and other laborers), transportation (ride-share drivers), and administration.

In a gig economy, businesses save a number of resources. First and foremost may be cash, but the gig economy also lets companies contract with experts who might be too high priced to maintain on staff for specific projects.

Consider a software developer. According to PayScale, the median annual salary for software developers with five years of experience is $112,921.

Meanwhile, according to Arc, formerly CodementorX, freelance software developers charge somewhere between $60 and $100 per hour, depending on experience. That can vary drastically by region. Arc surveyed 5,302 freelance developers from around the world in 2017 and found that gig workers in the least expensive regions cost between 30 percent and 40 percent less than those in the most expensive regions. But most freelancers charge between $60 and $100 per hour. That means a freelancer who works 1,790 hours a year (which the Organization for Economic Co-operation and Development said was the average in the United States in 2015) makes $107,400 to $179,000 per year. So hiring a full-time employee may be cheaper than hiring a gig-worker—if you stop at salary.

But you can't stop at salary because you also have to consider the cost of fringe benefits a company provides its full-time employees. In addition to the costs, a company's human resources staff incurs digging through résumés and interviewing candidates (often a months-long process), companies also provide a range of benefits, both cash and noncash. According to the Bureau of Labor Statistics, these include legally required benefits, such as Social Security; Medicare; unemployment insurance (8.5 percent); medical, dental, life insurance (7.6 percent); paid leave (6.7 percent), retirement savings, such as 401(k) matches (4.3 percent); annual bonuses (3.5 percent); supplemental pay; and overtime and premium (2.6 percent). Many employment specialists say you can add 30 percent in cash and noncash benefits to an employee's salary (in this case, $33,876). So a company that needs a software developer can expect to shell out $146,797 on salary and fringe benefits—meaning it may or may not save money by hiring a gig worker.

But wait, you can't stop even there because that calculation does not consider indirect costs, which are the expenses that a company incurs in its day-to-day operations, such as computer equipment, office supplies, and cleaning services. According to global enterprise resource planning (ERP) software provider Deltek, indirect costs include overhead and general and administrative (G&A) expenses (in addition to the fringe benefits discussed above). And companies spend an average of 25 percent and 18 percent of employees' salaries on overhead and G&A, respectively. If we break this down according to a full-time software developer's salary of $112,921, companies spend $28,230 on overhead and $20,326 on G&A expenses.

So now you have $112,921 + $33,876 + $28,230 + $20,326 = $195,353. The additional costs, which were not reflected in freelance software developer's annual salary, amounted to $82,432—73 percent of the software developer's annual salary. Suddenly, hiring a gig worker is much cheaper than hiring an employee.

But there are other benefits to hiring gig workers, and among them is the ability to contract for what you need and only what you need. Many businesses need help with projects that have a specific start and end and, for that, do not want to hire a freelancer year-round. Perhaps a company needs an annual report written or an app developed. Those would be good projects for gig workers, who can come in, get the job done, and be gone.

Hiring freelancers can also reduce what I call human resources (HR) costs—the expenses a company incurs when sorting through résumés, interviewing candidates, and conducting ongoing training. They do the latter longer than they should in many cases: due to the fear of being sued, companies often allow underperforming employees to stay when they should go. When hiring gig workers, these costs are not incurred. If a gig worker isn't a good fit—for any reason—a company can search for an instant replacement and do so with less bureaucratic and legal hassle than is involved in hiring a full-time employee.

Benefits of gig work—for gig workers

It's easy to assume that employers are somehow swindling the little guy from that analysis, but gig workers also benefit from a gig arrangement.

Simply stated, the gig economy provides more options for workers, and many are joining the gig economy not because they have to, but because they want to. I'm old enough to remember the days when "self-employed" meant "unemployed." Those days have long since passed.

Flexibility is one of the biggest draws of gig work. Freelancers can work from home—bringing in enough cash to pay the bills—while supporting younger children, caring for elderly parents, or pursuing other interests.

The rising gig economy also offers new inroads to previously unavailable career paths, thanks to low barriers to entry. In other words, gig workers can get a foot in the door and try new jobs for size. "Anyone who wants to can do microtasks," said Lukas Biewald, the CEO of CrowdFlower. "No matter their gender, nationality, or socioeconomic status, can do so in a way that is entirely of their choosing and unique to them."

Gig workers may also be attracted to the opportunity to earn more than they could in a traditional employment arrangement. While we've shown that it may be cheaper for a company to hire a gig worker, it's still possible for a gig worker to earn more than a full-time employee if that gig worker has low overhead (because he or she works from home, for example) and doesn't consider fringe benefits as pay (because he or she gets health insurance through a spouse, for example).

Lastly, the gig economy offers a safety net. Those of us who watched our parents work for a single company their entire lives only to be discarded when they were no longer valuable like having a variety of incomes sources and a backup plan. As a full-time gig worker, the loss of one gig isn't devastating because you have others. And as a temporary or part-time gig worker, the days of a mad scramble to find any job when full-time traditional employment falls through are gone. Gig work can take some of the anxiety out of job searching by giving workers an income to sustain them until they find the right new job.

According to QuickBooks, when 601 Uber drivers were asked if they would rather have a nine-to-five job with a set salary and some benefits, or a job where they had neither but could set their own schedule and be their own boss, 73 percent chose the latter. (Of course, they had already chosen the latter option by being Uber drivers, illustrating one flaw inherent in such studies—but the data point is still interesting since the drivers were being asked if they *would* take a steady job if one were available.)

In sum then, the gig economy can improve work-life balance and security for the gig workers. It's not surprising then that 60 percent of gig workers say they started freelancing by choice, up from 53 percent in 2014, according to "Freelancing in America: 2019." Today, many people view freelancing as much as a long-term career choice as they do a temporary way to make money—50 percent each.

Downsides of gig work

That said, gig work is not without challenges. According to "Freelancing in America: 2019," gig workers report fair pay, affordable health care, and retirement funding as key concerns.

In terms of pay, employers can avoid paying workers minimum wage or overtime by labeling them freelancers or independent contractors. Inconsistent income can also be a challenge. Maintaining enough work to ensure a stable income can be a continuous worry.

Indeed, many gig workers report the challenge of constantly looking for gigs, negotiating pay, and managing accounts as a key downside. It requires significant ongoing effort, which traditional employment does not. And that effort takes time away from the work that earns money.

Another downside to gig work is taxation. To support Social Security, employers and employees each pay 6.2 percent of wages up to the taxable maximum of $137,700 in 2020 while the self-employed pay the entire 12.4 percent themselves. Freelancers have the ability to take various tax deductions, but that may not make up the extra 6.2 percent Social Security hit.

Then there is the lack of fringe benefits—namely, health insurance and retirement funding.

The first is fairly clear cut—as a gig worker, you don't have access to an employer-sponsored medical plan or the cost savings that come with it, so you will have to buy health insurance through the Affordable Care Act, which can come with hefty premiums.

Self-employment also doesn't come with a built-in retirement plan. Gig workers then must determine how much they need to put away for retirement then find the right savings vehicle. That can be challenging, especially for those who have little experience in finance. But I'll discuss this topic more in the next section.

Now, there are some statistics that show gig workers are worse off than traditional workers. For example, according to "Freelancing in America: 2019," gig workers are more likely to have debt, including student loans (46 percent of gig workers versus 36 percent of traditional workers). They are also more likely to say they feel like they live paycheck to paycheck (59 percent of gig workers versus 53 percent of traditional workers). But this may reflect the younger age skew of gig workers more than the work arrangement itself, so I take that with a grain of salt.

What I can say with certainty is that gig work is better for some than others. According to Gallup, the gig economy is comprised of two types of gig workers: independent gig workers who have work autonomy and control, and contingent gig workers who experience work just like traditional employees but without the stability and benefits of a traditional job.

Chapter 2

Who Is Part of the Gig Economy?

If the fed cuts too much and too soon, it could stimulate an already bubbling inflation pot. This would almost ensure a recession.

—Mark Anthony Grimaldi, in January 2008; the global financial crisis officially started in December 2007

Gig workers don't fit a single profile, but looking at various studies, we can find some insights into the composition of the gig economy workforce.

Age

First, gig workers are likely to be younger than traditional workers. According to "Freelancing in America: 2019," more than 25 percent of workers were gig workers in every generation: 29 percent of baby boomers, 31 percent of Generation X, 40 percent of millennials, and 53 percent of Generation Z. And Generation Z, the most technologically sophisticated of the generations, freelanced more than any other generation of workers since the report's 2014 launch.

Interestingly, those who consider themselves freelancers tend to be older, whereas temp-agency workers and online-platform workers tend to be younger.[1] This is more evidence of the changing structure of gig work, which I discuss more later.

Gender

In terms of gender, the breakdown of the gig workforce varies. Some surveys report that there are more male than female gig workers; other surveys report the opposite.

This inconsistency may stem from the fact that men and women freelance in different ways. Men are much more likely than women to rely on gig work full-time while women are more likely to use it to earn supplemental income.[2] So whether men or women dominate depends on what is being studied.

It's also natural to assume that gig work may mirror full-time employment in terms of job function with more men in technical jobs (such as software development) and more women in nontechnical jobs (such as marketing). Etsy, for example, reports that women are particularly likely to sell goods online.[3]

Race

In terms of race, Gig Economy Data Hub—citing Edelman Intelligence—reports that the racial breakdown of the gig economy is similar to that of the overall workforce, but the story is nuanced. According to the US Bureau of Labor Statistics, gig workers in temp agencies and on-call jobs tend to be minorities (particularly Hispanic

---

1 Gig Economy Data Hub, from Edelman Intelligence, "Freelancing in America: 2017"; MBO Partners, "The State of Independence in America"; US Bureau of Labor Statistics, "Contingent and Alternative Employment Arrangements—May 2017"; American Action Forum and Aspen Institute's Future of Work Initiative, "The Gig Economy: Research and Policy Implications of Regional, Economic, and Demographic Trends"; JPMorgan Chase Institute, "The Online Platform Economy in 2018: Drivers, Workers, Sellers, and Lessors."

2 McKinsey Global Institute, "Independent Work: Choice, Necessity, and the Gig Economy."

3 Etsy, "Crafting the Future of Work: The Big Impact of Microbusinesses."

or African American), whereas other gig workers (independent contractors, freelancers, and consultants) tend to be Caucasian.

Education

Gig Economy Data Hub also reports that on most surveys, gig workers tend to be slightly more educated than the overall workforce. However, education varies by type of gig. Gig workers in some jobs (including temp-agency and on-call gigs) are less likely than the overall workforce to have a high school diploma. However, those gig workers who consider themselves freelancers, consultants, and independent contractors are more likely than the overall workforce to have a postgraduate degree.

Geography

Interestingly, given that many gig workers can do their jobs from anywhere, gig workers are more likely than traditional workers to live in an urban area, according to Gig Economy Data Hub, citing Edelman Intelligence. But there is a high concentration of these workers in Western states, particularly the San Francisco Bay Area. Given that this is the country's tech hub and many online platform companies got their start there, it shouldn't come as a surprise.

Skill and Pay

In terms of skill, freelancers are most likely to be skilled professionals, according to "Freelancing in America: 2019." The largest type of freelance work is skilled services (which includes information technology, marketing, and business consulting, to name just a few categories), which make up 45 percent of freelancers. Other types of freelancing include unskilled services (such ride-sharing, dog walking, and administrative tasks) at 30 percent or freelancers and selling goods (for example, on eBay or Airbnb) at 26 percent of freelancers.

According to "Freelancing in America: 2019," all gig workers have a median hourly rate of $20 an hour while those offering skilled services have a median hourly rate of $28 an hour. That compares to a median of $18.80 for the US overall. This means a skilled gig worker generally earns more per hour than a worker in the overall economy, at least in terms of cash income, but I'll have more to say about that later.

Politics

One final point: gig workers are more politically active than traditional workers. According to "Freelancing in America: 2019," 51 percent of gig workers say they are politically active; only 33 percent of traditional workers say the same. This may be because of gig workers' age (younger, as discussed above), or it may be because gig workers are particularly interested in making health care affordable since they cannot get it from their employers.

Chapter 3

Is the Gig Up or Here to Stay?

Some—but not all—companies have launched emergency policies to protect gig workers, who often don't receive sick pay or health benefits. However, many say the measures aren't enough.

—Center for Positive Organizations

Before COVID-19, the gig economy had an estimated value of $297billion and was expected to reach $455 billion by 2023, according to Statista. It was also growing fast, at three times the rate of the national workforce (8.1 percent versus 2.6 percent).

Then the pandemic struck. According to a Statista survey conducted in March 2020, at the start of the pandemic in the United States, 52 percent of global gig workers had lost their jobs due to the pandemic and another 26 percent had seen their hours decrease (perhaps because of a supply glut—according to HR consulting firm TalentRise, some areas of the gig economy tightened significantly as increased competition from laid-off employees swamped the market). And you know what happens when supply increases. According to Fairwork, those gig workers who were still working in March 2020 had, on average, lost two-thirds of their income.

But remember what I noted earlier about the Global Financial Crisis: uncertain times may actually drive gig work, not suppress it. By July 2020, GigSmart, a staffing company, said demand for its gig economy apps had increased by 25 percent since COVID-19 was declared a national emergency in the United States in March 2020. And many gig workers saw significant pay increases with the average GigSmart worker's hourly pay up from $17 an hour before COVID-19 to $22 an hour in July 2020. Several types of gig workers—warehouse laborers, handymen, and furniture movers—saw particularly significant pay increases.

Why? Because the labor market changed. We were all stuck at home. We weren't spending money by going out to eat and buying shoes and getting our hair colored; we were sitting on our sofas staring at our dingy walls and thinking, *Maybe I could finally get around to fixing those squeaky floorboards.* Many of us did home-improvement projects.

That raises another interesting point: COVID-19 may simply be changing the shape of the gig economy. Workers forced to stay at home began abandoning some gig services (such as ride-sharing and Airbnb) and increasing their use of others (such as grocery delivery services and home contractors). A 2020 survey by the University of Chicago Harris School of Public Policy and the Associated Press-NORC Center for Public Affairs Research showed just how drastically consumer attitudes change. Americans with higher incomes were more likely to use delivery services to help reduce their risk of infection, but 63 percent of people who previously used ride-sharing services had stopped doing so.

As I write this, the global economy is reopening and life is slowly returning to normal, but the long road ahead will undoubtedly be long. Before we get back to our old working lives, unemployment rates must continue to normalize and certainly will. But this could, once again, change the landscape for gig work.

But some things likely will not change. Technology will continue to keep us connected remotely and allow us to do our jobs more efficiently online. And our success at social distancing during the pandemic will likely have long-lasting effects on how and where we work with employees demanding remote work options and companies allowing them. All in, the stage is set for the gig economy to see sustained growth. The only point of contention is the location and extent of that growth.

Part 2

Thinking About Retirement as a Gig Worker

Chapter 4

What You Need to Know About Social Security (One Plus One Equals One!)

No greater tragedy exists in modern civilization than the aged, worn-out worker who after a life of ceaseless effort and useful productivity must look forward for his declining years to a poorhouse.

—Franklin D. Roosevelt

Ratchet up FICA (Social Security) tax contributions to the poverty level and raise the corresponding amount above the cap to make up the difference.

—Mark Anthony Grimaldi, *The Money Compass 2014*

The first thing to know as a gig worker pertains two Social Security, and there are two parts. First, a new gig economy worker usually says at tax time, "I didn't know I had to pay so much in taxes." Second, when planning for retirement, you can't rely on Social Security. Let's talk about all of that. How does Social Security work? Where is it headed? How will you as a gig worker participate?

Social Security—the origins

Before the Industrial Revolution in 1880, the United States was 72 percent rural. Most Americans were self-employed as farmers or laborers, and they lived in extended families that supported members who could not work. And that support didn't have to last long, given that life expectancy was short with the average American born in 1850 having a life expectancy at birth of only thirty-eight to forty years, depending on gender.

In only fifty years, that situation changed dramatically. By 1930, the United States was only 44 percent rural with the remaining 56 percent of the population residing in urban areas. At the same time, changes in public sanitation and health care, not to mention general living standards, increased life expectancies.

The Industrial Revolution, it seems, produced a population of Americans living into old age without the support of extended families. Suddenly, social insurance was critical.

At the time, the only federal precedent for social insurance in the United States was the Civil War pension program, under which the government paid union veterans and their surviving families. At the state level, many states had some form of a so-called "old-age pension" program, but these were generally inadequate; only about 3 percent of the elderly population received benefits, and the average benefit was about $19.50 per month (around $302 in 2020 dollars).

Social insurance became more pressing in the 1930s with the advent of the Great Depression. US unemployment rose to 23 percent, and families struggled to feed themselves. Fewer than 10 percent of American workers had an employer-sponsored private pension plan, so the elderly were particularly hard hit with most lacking sufficient income to be self-supporting.

There was a precedent for social insurance abroad: Germany created the first federal retirement system in 1889, and by 1935, more than twenty countries have operating social insurance systems. So with that as a basis; the US government set about creating its own social insurance.

The early days—relief, recovery, and reform

The origins of Social Security as we know it today date back to 1933 when Franklin Delano Roosevelt took office as president.

While his so-called "First New Deal," enacted from roughly 1933 to 1934, focused on relief and recovery from the immediate impacts of the Great Depression, his "Second New Deal," enacted from 1935 to 1937, sought to implement longer-lasting economic reforms.

Signed into law on August 14, 1935, the Economic Security Act is considered the starting point (and often defining initiative) of the Second New Deal. This bill (containing seven different programs) was debated in Congress for just eighteen days.

The original program—which eventually became known as Social Security—was designed to pay only the covered worker one-time retirement benefits at age sixty-five. To put that in perspective at the time, the remaining life expectancy for someone of that age was approximately twelve to fourteen years, depending on gender.

There were similarities to today's Social Security. Benefits were computed based on a worker's total cumulative wages, so the more years you were employed, the higher your benefit would generally be (although the calculation was also weighted so that workers with lower earnings received a proportionately higher benefit than workers with higher earnings).

But coverage was much more limited than it is today. Coverage under the program was based on occupation with most participants employed in "commerce and industry." Excluded groups included not just the self-employed but government (including military) employees, professionals (such as doctors and lawyers), non-profit employees, agricultural workers, and domestic help. As a result, only about half of US workers were covered.

The government began levying the payroll taxes that would fund the program in 1937 with the monthly benefit payments scheduled to start in 1942 (later changed to 1940)—a so-called "vesting period" that would build reserves before payments began flowing to beneficiaries.

But this arrangement presented a conundrum: what about workers who turned age sixty-five from 1937, when taxes were levied, until 1939, when benefits started? They would have contributed to Social Security but would not receive payments. To resolve this, the government agreed to make a one-time payment to people who turned sixty-five during this time.

A Cleveland, Ohio, streetcar operator named Ernest Ackerman was the first American who received these benefits, and thus the first person in the country to receive Social Security payment. He worked one day under Social Security—January 1, 1937—and earned a whopping $5. He paid five cents into Social Security and received seventeen cents back. Remember that for trivia night.

Evolution—enhancements and retrenchments

Since its early days, Social Security has evolved through more than ten major legislative enactments.

Some of them were enacted in 1939 before monthly benefits were even due to start. For example, one-time death payments were replaced with regular monthly survivor benefits, and dependent benefits were added. This was a significant expansion that is often considered the "second start" of Social Security in the United States because it changed the nature of the program. It transformed it from worker-based social insurance to family-based social insurance.

Other enhancements were enacted throughout the 1950s. For example, in 1950, the legislation raised the level of Social Security benefits by 77 percent on average. This was not a cost-of-living adjustment (COLA), but it established a precedent for the periodic raising of benefits to account for inflation. Later in the 1950s, disability legislation was adopted.

Then in 1972, two major bills greatly expanded the program. The first was a simple bill to raise the limit on the national debt (giving rise to automatic COLAs, which began in 1975 and contributed significantly to program costs). The second did much more: raised benefits for workers who postponed filing for Social Security (more on that later); provided a minimum benefit for workers with low lifetime earnings; expanded benefits to dependent grandchildren and widowers; offered reduced the disability benefit waiting period and offered Medicare coverage after two years of receiving disability benefits; created the Supplemental Security Income (SSI) program, which provides disability benefits to low-income individuals who either haven't worked or haven't earned enough work credits to qualify for traditional disability benefits; and more.

That was a major expansion but marked the approximate end of what is considered the expansionary period in Social Security policy making. That's because by the mid-1970s, serious financing problems had become evident in the Social Security program. Adverse economic conditions (remember "stagflation"?) led Social Security actuaries to report that the program was no longer in actuarial balance. From 1975 to 1981, the program was in an annual deficit, and the deficits were projected to continue for a decade. They still continue today, in fact. That is why the period since 1972 has been considered one of policy retrenchment versus expansion.

Social Security today

Social Security is still funded through the taxes that we, as US workers, pay into the system. As of June 2020, about 180 million people worked and paid Social Security taxes.

But your withholdings aren't being earmarked for you; they pay retirees and other beneficiaries who *currently* receive benefits. In fact, most of what you pay into Social Security pays for the benefits of current retirees and their surviving spouses and children. Only 15 percent helps people with disabilities.

How does it work? The current tax rate for Social Security is 6.2 percent for employers and 6.2 percent for the employees, or 12.4 percent total. As you pay Social Security taxes, you build credits in the program. The Social Security Administration increases the amount of money it takes to earn one credit annually. In 2021, for example, you receive one credit for each $1,470 of earnings up to the maximum of four credits per year. You generally need forty credits to become eligible for retirement benefits and building those will take about ten years.

The program is now massive. The amount of money coming into the Social Security system each year (more than $944 billion in the fiscal year 2019) is larger than the gross domestic product (GDP) of all but the world's sixteen richest nations. For most of the past twenty years, the Social Security program has been the largest single component of the federal budget. It accounts for about 5 percent of US GDP.

Now the fun part: the payout. The payments you receive from Social Security when you retire are calculated based on thirty-five years of earnings—your highest thirty-five years. It generally benefits you then to work longer so you can replace lower-earning years with higher-earning years.

That said, Social Security is not intended to be your sole retirement income. On average, it replaces only about 40 percent of pre-retirement income.

While that may seem insignificant, it is critical to keeping many Americans out of poverty later in life and also helps many others, including workers who become disabled and families in which the primary breadwinner dies. In the fiscal year 2019, Social Security paid about $892 billion in benefits to approximately 54 million beneficiaries per month, including 88 percent of the population aged sixty-five and older.

How it works

On to the big question: How much can you expect to earn from Social Security? That depends, as noted above, on your income (over your highest thirty-five years of earnings). It also depends on when you choose to start receiving benefits.

Full-retirement age—the age at which you can receive your full benefits—is between ages sixty-six and sixty-seven, depending on when you were born. The chart below illustrates:

Age at Which You Receive Full-Retirement Benefits

Year of Birth	Full Retirement Age
1943 to 1954	66
1955	66 and 2 months
1956	66 and 4 months
1957	66 and 6 months
1958	66 and 8 months
1959	66 and 10 months
1960 or Later	67

You can begin taking benefits at age sixty-two, but there's a catch. Your benefits will decline by half a percentage point for each month you begin before your full retirement age. Alternately, you can choose to postpone benefits until beyond your full-retirement age, in which case your benefits will increase. I'll discuss those options in more detail later.

For now, here's what you can potentially receive. According to the Social Security Administration (SSA), the maximum monthly Social Security benefit for a worker retiring at full retirement age in 2021 is $3,148. It's $2,324 for those retiring at age sixty-two and $3,895 for those retiring at age seventy.

Social Security also provides spousal benefits. You may be eligible if you're married or were (even if you're divorced, you may be eligible if your marriage lasted at least ten years, you haven't remarried, and your ex-spouse is sixty-two or older). The calculation works like this: If your retirement benefit is less than half of your spouse's or ex-spouse's retirement benefit, you get the larger amount. So let's say your spouse's retirement benefit if $1,500 per month and your own retirement benefit is $600 per month. Your spousal benefit would be $750 per month (half of your spouse's benefit).

Social Security also pays benefits to survivors. If your spouse has passed away, you can begin collecting his or her full retirement benefit at age sixty. That age declines in special circumstances. You can begin collecting at age fifty if you are disabled and immediately if you are caring for younger children (defined as those under age sixteen).

Other benefits

As noted above, though, Social Security is more than just a retirement program. It also pays disability benefits to Americans who can't work due to debilitating health issues. That said, the definition of disability is restrictive. You must expect the medical condition to last one year and/or cause your death, and it must prevent you from working at all (so no part-time or gig work allowed). A program called Social Security Supplemental Income also pays benefits to disabled adults and children with limited resources.

Social Security and the gig economy

A gig economy worker—also known as an independent contractor or a freelancer—has special Social Security considerations.

The first thing a new gig economy worker often says at tax time is, "I didn't know I had to pay self-employment taxes."

That's because a gig economy worker is responsible for taxes that an employer typically pays. The current tax rate for Social Security is 6.2 percent for employers and 6.2 percent for the employees, or 12.4 percent total. The current rate for Medicare is 1.45 percent for employers and 1.45 percent for employees, or 2.9 percent total. If you are an employee, you pay 6.2 percent + 1.45 percent, or 7.65 percent, and your employer pays the other half. But if you work for yourself, you'll pay both employer and employee taxes, a total tax rate of 15.3 percent. So, yes, you are not getting one of the top benefits of being an employee. That's because 50 percent of your Social Security benefits are funded by your employer. This benefit disappears for self-employed individuals. You are still required to make the full 15.3 percent FICA tax contribution, but now 100 percent of that must come from your paycheck. This makes Social Security much less appealing.

It's important to budget for these taxes when you begin gig work. How will you afford to pay them now out of your total earnings? But it's just as important to plan for your future. Economic security is a universal human need, and providing it is a challenge.

All societies have had to address this in some way, and in the United States, we do so through Social Security, which replaces a percentage of a worker's preretirement income based on his or her lifetime earnings and employer-sponsored 401(k) plans. As a gig worker, you'll receive the former (more on that later) but not the latter, so it's essential that you build a comprehensive gig economy retirement plan. I will show that in this book.

As mentioned above, the current tax rate for Social Security is 6.2 percent for employers and 6.2 percent for employees or 12.4 percent total. The current rate for Medicare is 1.45 percent for employers and 1.45 percent for employees, or 2.9 percent total. If you are an employee, you pay 6.2 percent + 1.45 percent, or 7.65 percent, and your employer pays the other half. But if you work for yourself, you'll pay both employer and employee taxes, a total tax rate of 15.3 percent.

On the bright side (if there's any bright side to taxes), you only pay into Social Security up to a certain amount of income—$142,800 in 2021. Once you hit that limit, your Social Security taxes don't increase when you add another job. And a special tax deduction for gig workers lets you deduct half of your self-employment tax to offset your income.

Plus, gig economy workers are still eligible for Social Security benefits. Your average lifetime earnings—used to calculate your Social Security payout—are based on your total earned income for each year. That includes both traditional W-2 jobs and 1099 jobs added together.

How does it work? Your annual earnings from gig work for Social Security purposes is the net profit from your Schedule C, so the money you deduced as business expenses don't count toward your Social Security record. For example, if you had $30,000 in gig earnings with $8,000 in deductible business expenses, your net profit is $12,000, and $12,000 gets added to your Social Security record for that year.

One caveat: You have to pay the taxes to get the benefit. Gig economy workers could shortchange themselves when it comes to their Social Security checks by not reporting their income accurately.

That means less goes to Uncle Sam now and less comes to the worker in retirement (not to mention, it's illegal). According to research funded by the Center for Retirement Research at Boston College, in 2014 alone, gig economy workers didn't pay $3.9 billion in Social Security contributions that they should have.

Take it or leave it?

Many people incorrectly assume that you can only start collecting Social Security benefits at ages sixty-three, sixty-five, sixty-seven, or seventy. This is totally false. You can file your paperwork to begin collecting at any time after your sixty-second birthday.

Many people automatically take Social Security benefits on schedule at age sixty-six but taking benefits as early age sixty-two or as late as age seventy may result in different payouts.

Some say to take Social Security as early as possible while others argue that the longer you wait, the higher your monthly check is. So do you take less per month today or wait and get more per month later?

Social Security calculates monthly payments so that total payments should be close to the same whether you take the money on time, early, or late. If you start taking benefits early, you'll receive smaller payments over a longer period of time. If you start taking benefits late, you'll receive bigger payments over a shorter time. In both cases, the end result should be the same as if you had started receiving benefits at normal retirement age.

Percentage of Full-Retirement Benefits You Will Receive

Age You Start Collecting	Full Retirement Age of 66	Full Retirement Age of 67
62	75%	70%
63	80%	75%
64	86.7%	80%
65	93.3%	86.7%
66	100%	93.3%

67	108%	100%
68	116%	108%
69	124%	116%
70	132%	124%

Note the use of the word "should" above. These calculations are based on your "normal" life expectancy. And life expectancies are averages.

So which option you choose may depend on two major factors: your life expectancy and whether you actually need the benefits to support your living expenses.

If you expect to live beyond your "normal" life expectancy, delaying benefits will result in higher monthly payments and a potentially higher lifetime total. In fact, for every year beyond your full retirement age that you delay collecting Social Security, your benefits will grow by about 8 percent. So if your full benefits would have been $2,000 per month, they would grow to $2,480 per month—a difference of $5,760 over a year.

On the other hand, if you don't expect to reach or exceed your life expectancy, it may make sense to start taking benefits as soon as possible—especially if you plan to invest your benefits because the return you receive on the invested money might make your total benefit greater than the increased benefits you'll receive if you take benefits on time or delay until age seventy.

When I'm asked when a retiree should start receiving benefits, my first question is, "Do you need the money to pay all your bills?" If the answer is yes, then start immediately.

If the answer is no, you must then ask, "At what age should I file so that I will get the most money during my lifetime?" To that, my response is always the same. All I need is the answer to one simple question, and I will tell you the exact date to file to ensure your maximum lifetime benefit. And that one simple question is: Tell me the date you are going to die. That's all I need to know.

Obviously, it's an unanswerable question. And that is the way the system is designed. Uncle Sam knows there is no way you can calculate your maximum benefit, and that is fine with him.

The future of Social Security

The future of Social Security is uncertain. According to the SSA's 2020 report, the projected actuarial deficit for the Social Security combined trust funds over the next seventy-five years is 3.21 percent of taxable payroll, 0.43 percentage point greater than the prior year.

The Old-Age and Survivors Insurance (OASI) Trust Fund alone can pay full benefits until 2034 and the combined OAS and Disability Insurance (DI) Trust Funds until 2035.

The main current causes, according to the SSA, are the repeal of the excise tax on employer-sponsored group health insurance premiums above a specified level (commonly referred to as the "Cadillac tax").

One can argue with that, after all, the US government isn't great at managing a budget. One can also debate the propriety of the wealth transfer. But one thing is certain: Without reform, the livelihood of much of the senior population is at risk.

On the eve of the program's creation, it was estimated that most American seniors lived in some form of economic dependency. By 1959, when official poverty measures were developed, poverty among the elderly was still at 35 percent. By the end of the twentieth century, poverty among the elderly was less than 10 percent. Clearly, Social Security has been central to America's way of life over the past seventy-five years. The program's future—along with its history—therefore ought to be of crucial concern to all Americans.

In summary, Social Security is not an entitlement; it is an investment. Contributions are made into the system in your name by both the employee and employer. The objective is to provide a base retirement for all Americans who participates in the program.

Is it a good investment? Many people have opinions.

Chapter 5

Evolution of Retirement Plans and the SECURE Act

The 401(k) was designed to supplement a traditional retirement, not replace them.

—Ted Benna, the father of 401(k) plans

The retirement industry has been trying to come up with innovative solutions for the way people work today (including the gig economy), and a new piece of legislation is just one example.

The Setting Every Community Up for Retirement Enhancement (SECURE) Act of 2019—which was signed into law on December 20, 2019, by President Donald Trump—makes it easier for small business owners to set up retirement plans that are less expensive and easier to administer.

There are some elements of the SECURE Act that help gig economy workers and some elements that don't. But here's what everyone needs to know about the SECURE Act.

The problem—low retirement savings

The US retirement system has been plagued by low savings rates for years (if not decades).

Social Security is simply not enough for most people. If you spent most of your life paying as much as possible into the system, and you retire in 2019 at age sixty-five, your monthly benefit will be $2,757. It jumps to $3,770 if you delay retirement until age seventy. That may sound nice; after all, it's more than $45,000 a year, which is certainly enough to live on in most locations. But that's not the norm. Most Social Security recipients receive $2,000 a month or less, and many receive even less than $1,000. The average benefit is $1,413, according to Social Security's latest fact sheet.[4]

As a result, Americans need to supplement Social Security with personal savings. But few are preparing to do so. According to 2018 data from the US Bureau of Labor Statistics (BLS), only 55 percent of adults participate in a workplace retirement plan, and those who do participate aren't saving enough. How bad is the situation?

Fifteen percent of Americans have no retirement savings at all, and 17 percent have between $1 and $74,999.[5]

The average 401(k) plan balance for all savers was $112,300 in the fourth quarter of 2019.[6]

The median 401(k) plan balance for those ages sixty-five and older is just $58,035.[7]

So Americans who are retiring have saved somewhere around $100,000, give or take. But most financial advisors recommend that Americans have at least $1million in their coffers at retirement. Why? Because that will kick off $60,000 per year in interest, assuming a 6 percent annual return. But really, $1million is just a start for the average person. Here's why.

First, that 6 percent rate of return is hypothetical and certainly not guaranteed. You could have some good years that add to your principal, but you could have some bad years with negative returns. Conservatively invested to avoid such swings, you would probably receive closer to a 3 percent to 4 percent return—and that barely

---

[4] Forbes.com, "The Average American Can't Save Enough to Retire," March 2019.

[5] Northwestern Mutual, "2019 Planning and Progress Study," May 2019.

[6] Fidelity Investments, press release, February 2020.

[7] Vanguard, "How American Saves 2019," June 2019.

outpaces inflation. (The long-term inflation average (1913 to 2018) is 3.15 percent annually.[8])

Second, even if you do manage to earn $60,000 from your $1million savings, that $60,000 may be taxed. If you are married and file jointly, you will pay 12 percent in federal income taxes, 7.65 percent in FICA taxes, plus state income taxes (as an example, 4.95 percent if you live in New York right now). That takes your $60,000 down to $48,781.[9]

Second, BLS research shows Americans close to retirement age spend about $66,000 annually per household on food, housing, clothing, transportation, health care, and other expenses.[10] So if you receive $48,781 after taxes and need to spend $66,000 to get by, you're almost $20,000 short.

I can't say emphasize enough that I'm not blaming Americans for this situation. Many people simply cannot afford to both live a typical middle-class lifestyle and, at the same time, save enough to finance a retirement that could last more than twenty years. Average weekly earnings for non-managers are $779, an almost forty-year high, meaning millions of Americans approaching retirement age spent their entire lives earning roughly $40,000 a year.[11]

Then there's the added complication of the gig economy. Traditional 401(k) plans—the mainstay of retirement planning—have typically not been available to freelancers. Plan eligibility is usually established by service requirements (a certain number of hours of work over a twelve-month period).

The solution—the SECURE Act

In a statement made after the SECURE Act bill passed the House of Representatives in May 2019, Rep. Richard E. Neal (D-Mass) said that it makes "significant progress in fixing our nation's retirement

8 Inflationdata.com.

9 Smartasset.com, Federal Income Tax Calculator, August 2020.

10 US BLS Consumer Expenditure Survey, September 2019.

11 Forbes.com, "The Average American Can't Save Enough to Retire," March 2019.

crisis and helping workers of all ages save for their futures." Does it? And what about freelancers? Let's look at the basic components of the SECURE Act.

Easier-to-offer 401(k) plans. Perhaps most importantly, the SECURE Act makes it easier for small businesses to set up 401(k) safe-harbor retirement plans.

A safe-harbor 401(k) plan is simply a type of 401(k) with an employer match that allows the employer to avoid most annual compliance tests. There's no need to go into the legal details; just know that the employer makes annual contributions on behalf of employees, and those contributions are vested immediately.

First, the SECURE Act increases the cap under which employers automatically enroll workers in safe-harbor retirement plans from 10 percent of wages to 15 percent.

Second, the SECURE Act provides a tax credit of up to $500 per year to employers who create a 401(k) or SIMPLE IRA plan with automatic enrollment. That means employees are automatically enrolled in the plan and must opt out of they don't want to participate.

As a freelancer, these elements of the SECURE Act benefit you in two ways.

First, many freelancers obtain the bulk of their business from smaller companies, and if smaller companies can more easily offer 401(k) plans, the freelancers who work from them can more easily participate (depending on employment categorization and hours worked—but more about that below).

Second, freelancers often transition into small business owners. Knowing you have an option to more easily offer competitive benefits to your future employees may help your business evolve.

Access for part-time employees. This is another big benefit of the SECURE Act. You can participate in a company's 401(k) plan if you're employed part-time. You just need to work either one thousand hours in a year (roughly half time) or have three consecutive years with five hundred hours of service per year (roughly quarter time).

Not all freelancers are employed part-time, of course. But some are. And some may consider it given this benefit. And by lowering the number of hours required for plan eligibility, the SECURE Act gives more workers access to workplace plans. Plus, perhaps in the future, a creative solution could allow freelancers access to these plans.

Changes in IRA contribution and withdrawal requirements. This component of the SECURE Act is nice, too, since freelancers are eligible for Individual Retirement Accounts (IRAs).

As you probably know, an IRA is an investment account that allows you to save for retirement on a tax-deferred basis. With a traditional IRA, you make contributions that are deductible on your tax return. Those contributions then grow tax-deferred until you withdraw them in retirement. And because many people are in a lower tax bracket in retirement than they were in preretirement, the money you accumulate may be taxed at a lower rate.

Roth IRAs are a little different. Money is taxed before you invest it but is not taxed when you withdraw it. There are reasons to choose a Roth IRA over a traditional IRA, and reasons not to, but those are beyond the scope of this chapter.

But back to the SECURE Act.

First, it changes IRA contribution rules. Previously, you had to be under age seventy and a half to contribute to a traditional IRA. Now, under the SECURE Act, anybody can make a traditional IRA contribution no matter his or her age. (This potentially allows a back door Roth IRA contribution, but that's another topic.) Of course, you still need to be able to demonstrate earned income, like from working at a job or self-employment.

Second, the SECURE Act pushes the age at which retirement plan participants must take required minimum distributions (RMDs) to seventy-two for those who were not seventy and a half by the end of 2019. It was previously seventy and a half. That means your money gets to grow tax-deferred for a year and a half longer than it did previously.

Withdrawals for student loan repayments. You've probably heard what a crisis student debt is becoming. Maybe you've experienced it yourself and are still struggling to repay your college loans, or maybe you have a child or grandchild in that situation.

The SECURE Act tries to address this problem by allowing the use of tax-advantaged 529 accounts for qualified student loan repayments of up to $10,000 annually.

A 529 plan is a college savings plan that may also be used to save and invest for K-12 tuition. You put money into the plan, invest it, and it grows. The money in a 529 plan may then be used to pay for educational expenses tax free. In other words, you don't pay taxes on the investment growth as you would if you invested the same money in a brokerage account or mutual fund.

This element of the SECURE Act means that during your lifetime, you can withdraw up to $10,000 from your 529 plan tax free in order to pay off student loan debt.

One caveat: Not all states may allow the student loan benefit of the SECURE Act to be tax free at the state level. You'll want to look into this before acting.

Annuity options. The SECURE Act encourages plan sponsors to offer annuities in retirement plans by reducing their liability if the insurer cannot meet its financial obligations. This isn't my favorite element of the SECURE Act because offering a tax-advantaged investment like an annuity inside of a tax-advantaged investment doesn't make a lot of sense. I'll leave it at that.

Other benefits. There are some other elements of the SECURE Act, like permitting Americans to make penalty-free withdrawals of $5,000 from 401(k) accounts to defray the costs of having or adopting a child. But I've covered the major ones, so let's move on to what it means.

The good

The bill makes progress in helping Americans beef up their retirement savings.

For example, reducing the number of hours that employees must work in order to participate in their company's 401(k) plan should help expand participation. Freelancers who can arrange a quarter-time or part-time work may benefit.

Additionally, the change in IRA contribution and RMD rules should provide a small boost to retirement savings for all Americans, freelancers included. Moving the starting age for RMDs to seventy-two certainly makes sense, given that people are living longer than they used to.

I also like that the SECURE Act allows you to use 529 plans to repay student loans. That's a great opportunity for individuals who have funds remaining in an educational savings account and want to put them to use.

The bad

I've already mentioned why I'm not a fan of the annuity option, and I should also mention that the SECURE Act removes something that is commonly referred to as a stretch IRA—an estate-planning strategy that applied to an IRAs inherited by a non-spouse beneficiary.

The stretch strategy allowed an IRA to be passed on from generation to generation, taking advantage of tax-deferred and/or tax-free growth of the assets within it. But the SECURE Act requires a full payout of the funds in the inherited IRA within ten years of the death of the original account holder. This will apply only to heirs of account holders who die starting in 2020.

That, incidentally, is how the government is paying for the SECURE Act provisions. The change to the stretch IRA is estimated to raise $15.7 billion in additional tax revenue.

But I digress. This provision of the SECURE Act immediately affects average Americans and not for the better. Let's say you inherited an IRA from someone other than your spouse. Under the old rules, you could withdraw money from the IRA over the rest of your life, meaning the money you didn't withdraw would grow tax free. But under the SECURE Act, you have to withdraw everything from the IRA within ten years. The money won't grow as long as it could, and you'll be paying taxes sooner than you might like. So if you saved a lot of money for retirement and plan to leave it to someone other than a spouse, you may want to rethink your strategy. The same is true if you are expecting to inherit an IRA.

The unknown

You thought this section was going to be "The Ugly," didn't you? I'm not that negative about the SECURE Act. I will say, however, that it is far from a cure-all for the nation's retirement challenges, especially for freelancers. And whether it ends up being a retirement game changer or not remains to be seen.

That said, as a freelancer, you can still take steps to save for retirement. According to T. Rowe Price, 33 percent of gig workers aren't saving anything for retirement—22 percent because they don't have access to a traditional workplace 401(k) plan and 11 percent by choice. Don't be in that category for any reason. How?

As mentioned above, traditional and Roth IRAs are great options for freelancers. The annual contribution limit for 2020 is $6,000 ($7,000 if you're age fifty or older), though it phases out at certain income levels.

You may also consider a Simplified Employee Pension (SEP) IRA, which is available to anyone with a freelance income. Freelance workers can put up to 25 percent of net earnings or $57,000 (whichever is less) into a SEP-IRA each year. Contributions are tax-deductible as with a traditional IRA.

You could also consider a Solo 401(k), which is a 401(k) plan for one person. As with a workplace 401(k) plan, as an employee, you can contribute up to $19,500 per year ($26,000 if you're fifty or older). But since you're both employer and employee on this plan, you can also make contributions as an employer (basically matching yourself), so your total contribution may be up to $57,000 each year.

Chapter 6

How to Open a Gig Retirement Plan

The trouble with retirement is that you never get a day off.

—Abe Lemons

Retirement income is like water in a swimming pool. If you do nothing, it will evaporate and not be there when you jump in.

—Mark Anthony Grimaldi

Now that we've established that you can't rely on Social Security and discussed the SECURE Act, let's get into a topic about which I have some expertise: retirement planning. As a gig worker, you don't have the luxury of an employer-sponsored retirement plan to help ensure your financial future, and a traditional 401(k) plan is likely out of your reach given the administrative costs associated with creating and maintaining one.

But you do have some options. I'll list them in the order of good, better, and best.

Individual Retirement Account (IRA)—good

The simplest vehicle is the IRA, either a traditional IRA or Roth IRA. Very little setup is required. Gig workers can contribute up to $6,000 per year in 2020, $7,000 if age fifty or older (subject to income phaseouts).

- Advantages—initial tax deduction, easy setup
- Disadvantages—taxed at retirement, low contribution limits

Solo 401(k)—good

Lastly, gig workers can choose a self-employed or solo 401(k). Designed for those who are solo business owners—essentially self-employed with no employees or their only employee is their spouse—the solo 401(k) allows you to maximize contributions because it considers you both employer and employee.

It does involve some setup and maintenance: in addition to adopting a formal plan document, you'll need to file paperwork with the IRS each year once you accumulate $250,000 in your account.

As an employee, you can contribute up to 100 percent of your compensation up to an annual maximum of $19,500 in 2020 ($26,000 if you're fifty or older). As an employer, you can make additional profit-sharing contributions. Total contributions from both the employer and employee cannot be more than $57,000 ($63,500 if you're fifty or older).

- Advantage—initial tax deduction, high contribution option
- Disadvantages—taxed at retirement, high administration costs, contributions can't come from multiple sources.

SEP-IRA—better

Gig workers who have greater needs and are a bit more sophisticated in terms of retirement planning can also choose a SEP-IRA.

Essentially, SEP-IRAs are employer-funded retirement plans; employees make no contributions. In 2020, the contributions you make to each employee's SEP-IRA (including your own) cannot exceed the lesser of 25 percent of compensation or $57,000.

The plan is easy to set up and maintain, and there are no setup fees or annual charges. SEP-IRAs are great for gig workers who have few or no employees and aren't sure they will be able to contribute to the plan every year.

- Advantages—initial tax deduction, high contribution option
- Disadvantages—taxed at retirement, contribution can't come from multiple sources

Roth IRA—better

Roth IRAs are similar to traditional IRAs with the biggest difference between how they are taxed. Roth IRAs are funded with after-tax money, unlike traditional IRAs, which are funded with pre-tax money. That means contributions are not tax-deductible. Upon retirement, however, distributions are tax free (unlike traditional IRAs), provided an array of conditions are met.

- Advantage—not taxed at retirement
- Disadvantages—low contribution limits, five-year vesting requirement

Brokerage account—best

A brokerage account is nothing more than an account with a brokerage firm. Charles Schwab, Vanguard, Fidelity, and E*TRADE are just a few brokers that offer brokerage accounts free of charge.

These accounts are called "brokerage" accounts because they allow the purchase and sale of investments products such as stocks, bonds, mutual funds, and exchange-traded funds (ETFs).

Why is this your best choice? Because with this type of account, all the items on my "RetireSmart GIG Retirement" wish list are possible. Yes, every single one!

Advantages:

- Has no contribution limits
- Has no investment choice limitations
- Let's you touch your money when you need it most
- Knows the tax difference between income and capital gains
- Has no age restrictions on your money
- Has no distribution minimums
- Understands the tax code
- Has no 10 percent excise taxes on distributions
- Has no 1099Rs
- Has no administration expenses
- Can be funded from any source
- Has no CPA expenses
- Has no vesting requirements

Disadvantage:

- Contributions are taxed after the standard deduction is reached at $12,950

Now that you know which type of account offers the most advantages, you will need a financial professional to build and manage a prudent portfolio. Unless, of course, you have the skill set to do it yourself.

Please keep in mind that day trading is not a prudent portfolio. Cryptocurrency is not a prudent portfolio. Buying the stocks that the talking heads are touting online or on TV is not a prudent portfolio. In fact, I proved in my first book, *The Money Compass*, that holding five blue chips is not a prudent portfolio. In chapter 9, I will share my secret for creating and managing a well-diversified portfolio that withstands the test of time. It's almost so simple that you'll think there has to be more to it. Trust me, you will see for yourself.

But first, here are the ways to go about selecting a quality financial advisor.

What about financial advisors?

The question many of you may ask is, "Do I need a financial advisor to help with this?" The answer is "Maybe." It depends on the advisor.

I certainly don't want to leave you to your own devices. No offense, but how many people can manage their monthly budget properly, let alone their retirement nest egg? I also don't want to leave you to the wolves of Wall Street. So I'm going to use my more than thirty years of experience and lay out a GPS for choosing a financial advisor who is right for you.

My advice to you is to ask someone in your life who seems financially secure whom they use. Trust me when I say this person will be flattered that you came to him or her for advice. And you'll probably get a good referral. Successful people network with each other, so the odds are the person you go to (assuming he or she is as financially secure as you believe) will have the name of a financial advisor to share.

This approach is rooted in something my dad used to say when I was growing up. "Kids, let me give you some advice. Never take advice from someone less successful than you."

I don't know if he coined that expression or borrowed it from someone else, but it's dripping with wisdom.

Once you have the name of a financial advisor (or a few), your work isn't over. You'll still need to do some due diligence, and I'm going to explain how. Before we start, however, let me clarify what I mean by "financial advisor."

In contrast to stockbrokers (who help you trade stocks), insurance agents (who help you buy life insurance and annuities), and accountants (who prepare your taxes), financial planners often advise their clients on how to save and invest their money. Whether you want help with a specific financial goal or need a broad analysis of your investments, a financial planner can help. Some even specialize in certain areas, such as retirement planning and estate planning.

Got it? Great. Here's how to find one.

Step 1: choose a type of financial advisor

Anyone can hang out a shingle as a financial planner, but you can break financial advisors down into two major groups based on how they are paid: commission-based advisors and fee-only advisors. But note that there are many hybrid advisors that charge both a commission and a fee. Try to avoid them, if possible, because they may have too many masters to answer to, and you will probably not be one of them.

Commission-based advisors. Commission-based advisors sell financial products—mutual funds, annuities, and insurance, for example—and receive commissions on those products.

They are sometimes referred to as "registered representatives" because they have their Series 6 or Series 7 license from the Financial Industry Regulatory Authority (FINRA), and they are often employed by large financial institutions.

Because some or all of a commission-based advisor's income is determined by what he or she sells you, many people consider them to have a conflict of interest. Do they want to sell you a mutual fund because it's what's best for you, or because it offers them the highest commission?

These professionals—and there are many excellent ones out there—are regulated by a standard called "suitability." This means that they are always required to recommend investments products they are confident are suitable for you.

Usually, they make this judgment after they complete a "getting to know your client" questionnaire. While there is no uniform process for this exercise, most advisors have a series of questions for you to answer that help shape your investment horizon, risk tolerance, and experience. The good advisors will have you update this form periodically—once a year is usually sufficient.

A problem can arise when the advisor has a choice of two "suitable" investments. What prevents them from selecting the one that pays a higher commission? Remember, their obligation is to suitability and really nothing else. If they meet that standard, they aren't required to pick the best option. This can create distrust in the relationship between the client and advisor.

Fee-only advisors. Fee-only advisors make money not through commissions but through flat fees—sometimes hourly rates, sometimes a percentage of the assets they manage. For example, you might pay $1,500 for a financial plan, or you might pay 1 percent of all the assets—investment and other accounts—they're managing for you. Often, fee-only advisors provide more comprehensive advice than commission-based advisors do, including asset allocation, retirement planning, and estate planning, to name just a few areas.

This type of professional is known as a fiduciary. A fiduciary has a different and perhaps higher burden than a non-fiduciary (such as an advisor bound by suitability). Where the commission-based advisor must only recommend investments that are suitable, the fee-only advisor must select investments based on the "best interest" of the client. This is a higher and more difficult standard to reach.

In fact, the SEC has issued specific criteria spelling out what it considers to be the "best interest" standard. First and foremost, the advisor must eliminate, or at least expose, all conflicts of interest that might incline the advisor to render advice, which is not disinterested. I am very familiar with this firsthand because, as a fee-only advisor, I also manage a no-load mutual fund. So I must disclose in clear and simple language that I am compensated to perform my advisor duties, but I should recommend that a client use the fund I manage I will receive compensation for the additional service I am providing.

What's the Difference? If it's not yet obvious, the major difference between a commission-based advisor and a fee-only advisor is that commission-based advisors sell products and fee-only advisors provide a service. The fee-only advisor has four specific duties:

1. Duty to provide advice that is in the best interest of the client
2. Duty to seek the best execution (which means getting the client the best price possible)
3. Duty to provide advice and monitoring over the course of the relationship
4. Duty of loyalty (which means the advisor must put the client's interest above his or her own)

I think you can see then why I'm an advocate of fee-only financial advisors.

Step 2: determine what your advisor will do

Whether you want help with a specific financial goal (such as preparing to buy a house) or need a broad analysis of your investments, a financial planner can help. Some specialize in estate planning; others consult on a comprehensive array of financial issues. But essentially, you can look at their services in three ways.

You will want a consultation from an advisor who charges an hourly fee if you have specific questions about a specific financial problem, such as buying a house, going back to school, or selling a business.

If you need an advisor to create a one-time road map that will help you reach your financial goals—from insurance to investments—you're looking for comprehensive financial planning.

Finally, if you're looking for asset management—someone to allocate your portfolio and keep it balanced over time—you will want a long-term financial partner. He or she will invest and manage your money, providing continuous updates as your circumstances change as well as comprehensive reporting.

Step 3: locate some options

Next, you'll want to obtain a short list of advisors. One place to find an advisor is through the National Association of Personal Financial Advisors (www.napfa.org), a nationwide organization of fee-only advisors. You can also look on the CFP website (home of Certified Financial Planners—more on that later). You can also ask for referrals from your accountant, attorney, colleagues, or friends.

Step 4: review the candidates' credentials

Once you have a short list, you'll want to review credentials. Anyone can call himself or herself a financial advisor and may tack on a combination of letters after their names. How do you make sense of it?

CFP, short for Certified Financial Planner, is a significant credential. Advisors must have several years of experience, pass a six-hour exam administered by the Certified Financial Planner Board of Standards about the specifics of personal finance, and complete continuing education. They are also held to strict ethical standards.

Even with a CFP designation, you'll want to look at experience. How long has the advisor been in practice? What was their previous experience? Education is important, as is practice.

Finally, consider fit. Advisors have different styles and philosophies. Does the advisor's style mesh with yours? Most advisors will provide a free initial consultation to tell you about their practice. After that conversation, do you like and trust your advisor? It's a close (and in many cases, long-term) relationship, and your financial advisor will know many personal details of your life.

Step 5: meet the advisor face-to-face or through Zoom

Meeting with your advisor face-to-face is important, but I realize in today's world, it's not always possible. But even if you can't meet in person, don't hire a financial advisor based on a slick website or several emails. Try to engage in a meaningful dialogue.

A good financial advisor will do more listening than talking. He or she will not offer you any solutions before getting to know you and your financial objectives.

Although the Securities and Exchange Commission (SEC) doesn't allow financial advisors to advertise via client testimonials, it is certainly fine to ask the advisor for three references. In fact, I'd ask for several: one from a long-term client of ten years or longer, one from a short-term client of less than one year, and one from a client that is similar to you in his or her objectives and time horizon.

Finally, ask the financial advisor the most important question there is: What is their track record? This is a tricky question because the SEC has strict rules about what a financial advisor can claim as a track record. But he or she should be able to provide you with something.

If a financial advisor chosen based on the steps above can readily provide you with three references and a track record, and you get a good feeling about the person, you may have found your trusted partner.

Let's make this easy

In summary, there are two steps. First, choose the type of account that you feel works best for you. I strongly recommend a brokerage account for its convenience, low cost, a wide array of investment choices, and tax efficiency. Second, choose an investment advisor. I think you will be best served by one that adheres to strict fiduciary guidelines—a fee-only advisor.

Part 3

Step-by-Step Guide to a Gig Retirement

Chapter 7

Three Steps to a Secure Tax-Free Gig Retirement

Compound interest is the eighth wonder of the world. He who understands it, earns it… He who doesn't…pays it.

—Albert Einstein

The system is rigged, but you can beat it. How? In this chapter, I will show you—in three easy steps—how to create a secure gig retirement that is taxed at the lowest possible federal rate, eliminating the cancer that eats away at your nest egg in your golden years. Each step is simple, and anyone can take it. But the sooner you attack the problem, the better the outcome.

Understanding the standard deduction

Let's start by talking about how you put money away for retirement—not about how you invest it, but how it goes into your account after you earn it.

To create a low-tax secure retirement, the first and most important step is the type of account you open. Retirement money usually is deposited into a 401(k) plan or IRA after taxes. This approach is completely wrong.

Here's where I break away from the traditional retirement propaganda that you must have a qualified retirement account to save for retirement. That's the bait, and here's the switch:

The powers that be entice you with the promise of a tax deduction today that will make your life better today, they don't address your tomorrow. And trust me, all of our tomorrows come.

In 2017, when they changed the standard deduction to $12,000 (now $12,950), it was a game changer for the retirement industry—at least for smart folks who were paying attention.

The standard deduction is one of the three core tenets of my book, and it's very simple to understand. All Americans are entitled to an individual standard deduction of $12,950. In simple terms, this means that if you make that amount or less, you will pay $0 in the city, federal, and state income taxes. That's right, I said $0. Not one penny.

And we can use that to our advantage. You can save up to that amount in an after-tax brokerage account each year. That means that it will be tax-free money that the IRS will treat exactly the same as after-tax money. That means, at retirement, you will be able to withdraw that $12,950 tax free because, according to the IRS, you used your standard deduction at the time of deposit.

Why is this better than a Roth IRA? Because the maximum contribution to a Roth is only $7,000, and that comes with hundreds of pages of IRS regulations—hoops you must jump through in order to get your money out tax free.

So in this chapter, when I lay out your three-step plan, when I'm discussing growing money after tax, I'm referring to using the standard deduction in a very smart way.

I should also note that that standard deduction applies to a person, not a household, so if you are filing a joint return, each wage earner gets the full standard deduction.

Three steps to a secure low-tax retirement

Step 1: grow your portfolio after taxes.
Step 2: pay off debt.
Step 3: save your age divided by three.

Step 1: grow your portfolio after taxes. It's this simple: start saving today with after-tax money. After-tax money is your paycheck, and you should put a portion of it in a brokerage account.

How? Just contact any one of the large investment companies—Vanguard, Schwab, or Fidelity—and ask to open a regular brokerage account in your name. Most companies don't charge a fee to open or maintain this type of account.

Then ask to set up an automatic investment program in which you will invest a certain amount each month. How much depends on your individual financial circumstances.

As to where to invest the money, Warren Buffet has said that if he weren't managing his own money, he would put 90 percent in a low-cost S&P 500 Index mutual fund. Who am I to argue with one of the greatest investors in history?

My biggest problem with his suggestion is that it offers no downside protection. If the market loses 5 percent, you lose 5 percent. If the market goes down 15 percent, your account does also. In 2008, the stock market lost nearly 40 percent, as did the low-cost S&P 500 funds. Ouch!

I know many are asking, "What's the big deal? The market bounced back." That's easy to say after the fact, but human emotions take over during a market crisis and bad decisions are made. I still come across experienced investors who tell me they sold after the 2000 tech bubble burst and didn't get back in until after the rebound. Other sold after the global financial crisis drop and/or the COVID-19 collapse.

If you need proof, here it is: During the first quarter of 2020, which is when COVID-19 hit, the Vanguard Investments experienced its first quarterly net outflows in a decade. It was also the largest outflow Vanguard has ever experienced. So did the money flow in during the second quarter? Nope—another negative net outflow. The third and fourth quarters of 2020 were also negative. Thousands of experienced investors controlling billions of dollars panicked and sold at the exact wrong time.

Why are you any different? Maybe you are. I hope you are. But it's my goal to make you a better investor. My bigger point, however, is that although I am a fan of low-cost S&P 500 funds, I think Mr. Buffet would agree that greater diversification is needed when building and maintaining a prudent secure retirement portfolio.

Later in this book, I reveal my tried and true secret for building a secure retirement portfolio the US government will work to ensure is healthy and prosperous. But first, let's talk about how investing a small amount of money on a regular basis will work to your advantage over time.

Dollar-cost averaging

Making small investments at regular intervals over time—called dollar-cost averaging—can be an effective investment strategy. It establishes discipline, and by helping you to invest regularly, it can alleviate any worries trying to time the market.

It can even help you take advantage of market fluctuations. Because you invest the same dollar amount each period, you typically purchase more shares when prices are low and fewer shares when prices are high. This means that over the entire purchase period, your average cost per share could be lower than the investment's average price per share. Paying less than the average share price is desirable because it allows you to purchase more shares over time.

What does that mean? First, let's define the terms I just used.

Your average cost per share is the amount you invested divided by the number of shares you received. So if you invest $5,000 over five purchases and receive a total of 788 shares, your average cost per share is $5,000 divided by 788 or $6.35.

The average share price is the total price of the shares you bought divided by the number of purchases you made. So if you make five purchases—at $5 a share, $6 a share, $7 a share, $8 a share, then $9 a share—your total share price is the sum of these numbers or $33. The average share price is $33 divided by the total number of purchases or five—so $6.60.

Now that you know the terms, it may be helpful to look at a few hypothetical examples to illustrate how dollar-cost averaging works. Let's say that you've decided to invest $5,000 in an equity mutual fund by making $1,000 investments per quarter over a five-quarter (fifteen-month) period. How will three typical market environments—rising market, declining market, and volatile market—affect your investment?

Rising Market

Investment	Amount	Share Price	Shares Acquired
First quarter	$1,000	$5	200
Second quarter	$1,000	$6	167
Third quarter	$1,000	$7	143
Fourth quarter	$1,000	$6	167
Fifth quarter	$1,000	$9	111
Total	$5,000	$33	788

Average share cost to you ($5,000/788 shares): $6.35 Average share price ($33/5 purchases): $6.60

Declining Market

Investment	Amount	Share Price	Shares Acquired
First quarter	$1,000	$5	200
Second quarter	$1,000	$3	333
Third quarter	$1,000	$3	333
Fourth quarter	$1,000	$2	500
Fifth quarter	$1,000	$1	1,000
Total	$5,000	$14	2,366

Average share cost to you ($5,000/2,366 shares): $2.11 Average share price ($14/5 purchases): $2.80

Volatile Market

Investment	Amount	Share Price	Shares Acquired
First quarter	$1,000	$5	200
Second quarter	$1,000	$7	143
Third quarter	$1,000	$5	200

Fourth quarter	$1,000	$3	333
Fifth quarter	$1,000	$5	200
Total	$5,000	$25	1,076

Average share cost to you ($5,000/1,076 shares): $4.65 Average share price ($25/5 purchases): $5.00

As you can see, not only does dollar-cost averaging work in any market environment, it also works for any type of investor with any amount of money to invest.

If you don't have much to invest, dollar-cost averaging can be a great way to ease into investing because you can start with a relatively small amount of money.

And if you have a large sum to invest (such as an inheritance), you can put the money into a savings or money market account then move small portions into a stock or bond mutual fund over time.

And that's it. You're on your way to growing your portfolio with after-tax money—step 1. Well done! Now let's look at step 2.

Step 2: pay off debt. Paying off debt is as important as anything you can do to put yourself in the best possible position for a secure retirement—and to achieve it, you'll need to figure out how much you owe and when you will be debt free if you keep making the same payments you're currently making.

To make this determination, there are many free debt calculators online. My favorite is Bankrate.com. Try it, then consider this:

If your debt is paid off prior to your projected retirement date, that's great. Keep doing what you're doing.

But if your debt payment extends into your retirement, then you must do one of two things: either increase your monthly debt payments or push your retirement date off until your debt is paid off.

As I always say, you can't retire until your debt retires.

Step 3: save your age divided by three. As a practicing economist for more than thirty-five years, I've looked at every possible way to advise my readers about the easiest and most accurate way to figure out how much money they should save for their retirement.

For clarity, when I refer to saving for retirement, I mean saving enough money to live essentially the same lifestyle after retirement as you did before retirement—not 80 percent of your current income, as some advisors will tell you. You don't want to cut back.

I can't tell you how upset I get when I walk into Walmart, Target, or McDonalds and see older folks working physically demanding jobs. I understand that some people just love to work and need to stay busy. I understand that others look at the paycheck they receive from such jobs as a way to cover some fun extras in their life. But I believe the majority of retirees would rather be home with their spouses, children, grandchildren, and even great-grandchildren than working near-minimum-wage jobs.

So when I see that happening, I wonder, *What went wrong in those folks' lives to put them in the position to have to work those jobs?*

I would love to sit down, buy them a cup of coffee, and listen to their story, but I'm pretty sure most of them would tell me the same thing—that they had no idea that retirement would sneak up on them so fast, and that they didn't know how much to save for the future.

Don't want that to be you? Well, I can't slow down time, but I can tell you how to calculate exactly how much you'll need to save to put yourself in the best possible position for a comfortable retirement. Are you ready?

Here it is. Don't blink or you'll miss it because it's simple.

Take your age, divide it by three, and save that percentage of your gross salary.

That's it. That's the secret sauce. Don't believe me? Here's an example.

Let's look at a twenty-five-year-old woman (I know, you likely aren't that young, but this is just an example. You'll see why I used a young age shortly).

This young woman earns the median US salary of $59,039. Her age divided by three is 8.33 percent, and 8.33 percent of $59,039 is $4,918. So she'll need to save $4,918 per year to get on the path to secure retirement.

Don't believe me? By age sixty-five, this twenty-five-year-old woman will accumulate enough assets to create an income stream of $73,537. Add this to the median Social Security benefit for a sixty-five-year-old individual—$16,848 annually—and this saver will have a gross annual income of $90,385, which is $59,039, adjusted for inflation. (That means $87,331 gives this saver the same buying power as $59,039 did when she was twenty-five.)

Now, let's look at another saver, a thirty-five-year-old man who waited until he was thirty-five to start saving for retirement. He also earns the median US salary of $59,039.

If you're like most of my readers, you probably think thirty-five is relatively young to begin saving for retirement. And it is. But this young man will pay a procrastination penalty for waiting those ten years.

The penalty is easy to determine. Start with age thirty-five and divide it by three, which gives us 11.67 percent. Since the age is higher, the percentage this young man must save is also higher.

You may think that's not too bad. This young man waited ten whole years to start saving, and he only has to save about 3 percent more than he would had he started at age twenty-five.

But this is where the majority of Americans make a fatal error that causes them to be working well into their seventies and eighties. They don't account for the procrastination penalty.

What is the procrastination penalty? It's the 8.33 percent this young man should have started saving at twenty-five. He has to add this percentage to his current savings rate of 11.67 percent, meaning he has to save roughly 20 percent of his gross annual income. That's quite a penalty!

And it compounds. Taking it a step further, a forty-five-year-old woman who just started saving for retirement would have to save 15 percent of her gross income, plus the 11.67 percent she should have started saving at age thirty-five, plus the 8.333 percent she should have started saving at age twenty-five. That's roughly 35 percent of her gross income!

It's a tough pill to swallow, but if you do this and earn a competitive return on your savings, in thirty years, you'll be shopping at Macy's instead of working at Walmart.

I realize everyone reading this chapter knows that the longer you wait to save, the longer you have to save. What I'm hoping to accomplish here is to lay out, in simple mathematical terms, how much waiting actually costs you.

Try this calculation for your age; you'll see that it works.

My hope is that this doesn't discourage older Americans from saving because they can't reach their goals. Anything you can save today will make your life better tomorrow. But aim high—aim for your retirement GPS, which, in summary, is this:

Step 1: grow your portfolio after taxes.

Step 2: pay off debt.

Step 3: save your age divided by three.

That's all there is to it. There's no magic. If you follow these steps, you'll achieve the most secure lowest-tax retirement possible.

That's what the rich do. They don't have 401(k) plans; they create all of their wealth with after-tax dollars.

As a side note, they then take advantage of the extremely attractive capital gains tax rate, and they pass their wealth to the next generation virtually tax free using the step-up in cost basis. I know those are some new ideas, and I'll explain them all later.

For now, however, just remember this: If you think the tax system is tilted in favor of the rich, just remember who created it—the rich. And as long as the rich use their wealth to gain and keep power, that will never change. And if the system will never change, the only thing that can change is you.

Chapter 8

How *Not* to Invest a Gig Retirement Plan

A lot of people become pessimists from financing optimists.

—C. T. Jones

Before moving on, I'd like to say a word (actually, many words) about how *not* to invest in a gig retirement plan. It's simple: Don't be the target!

Target-date retirement funds—the lie inside the lie

A large problem is brewing in most Americans' retirement plans. It's a problem that is hidden in plain sight by some very clever marketing. It's a problem so big that the only way to fix it is to break federal securities law. Wall Street knows about it, the US government knows about it, and now you, the target of the problem, will know about it.

The lie: "Set it and forget it" works.

In this chapter, I plan to expose target-date retirement funds as gimmicks whose popularity far overshoots their effectiveness. I will expose them as ticking time bombs (with misleading fees) that are actually acting counter to their intended purpose by adding risk as time goes by.

What is a target-date retirement fund?

Very simply, a target-date retirement fund, also called a target-date fund, is a fund that automatically rebalances its holdings to become more conservative as an investor gets closer to retirement. These funds are designed for investors who prefer to put their portfolios on autopilot. They are perhaps the lowest-maintenance retirement-saving product you can purchase. And that's exactly what makes them so popular. With a target-date fund, you can set it and forget it, so to speak.

Who do target-date retirement funds target?

You, that's who.

Let me tell you a story about a woman who wrote to me in 2013 about an experience she had investing in target-date funds, which, as I've noted, automatically rebalance their assets to become more conservative as an investor gets closer to retirement.

In 2005, Jane Doe, as I'll call her to protect her privacy, received a large inheritance from her parent's estate. Having no experience managing a six-figure portfolio, Jane asked for recommendations, and friends suggested she call one of the large national investment firms. Jane did so, speaking to a client-service representative who asked questions designed to determine Jane's investment experience, investment horizon, and tolerance for risk—much what you'd expect of any financial professional.

"At the time, I was fifty-seven years old, and I thought that this inheritance would put me on pace to retire at age sixty-five," recalls Jane, a single mother and the sole breadwinner in her family, who had previously handled all of her own retirement planning, placing other investments in very conservative mutual funds.

The client service representative Jane spoke to told her that a target-date fund would be a fantastic choice and explained why.

First, the target date, the client service representative explained, refers to a target retirement date and often is part of the name of the fund. For example, you might see target-date funds with names such as Retirement 2030 Fund or Target 2030 Fund, which would be designed for individuals who intend to retire during or near the year 2030.

The client service representative also told Jane that target-date funds offer a long-term investment strategy based on holding a mix of stocks, bonds, and other investments that automatically shift as the participant ages. For example, a fund's initial asset allocation, when the target date is years away, might consist primarily of stocks, which have greater return potential but also greater volatility. As the target date approaches, the fund's asset allocation might shift to include a higher proportion of more conservative investments, such as bonds and cash, which generally are less volatile. "As a novice, I thought that this was a very prudent approach," says Jane.

That's a thought echoed by other purveyors of target-date funds. "They're an excellent investment solution for most people in most situations," said one financial planner at T. Rowe Price, which offers a full menu of target-date funds, quoted in the media. "I liken them to being the automatic transmission of the investing world—and 95 percent of cars sold in North America have automatic transmission."

Since Jane's desired retirement date was 2013, when she turned sixty-five, the client service representative recommended that Jane split the assets between two funds, one with a target retirement date of 2010 and one with a target retirement date of 2015. Jane agreed and was thrilled with her decision. "When the call was finished, I was filled with confidence and was very proud of myself for selecting a combination of two funds that would be managed in accordance with my risk and retirement in mind," she says.

Jane's investment strategy worked well for a few years, but then the financial crisis hit. In 2008, the fund with a target retirement date of 2010 lost 20.67 percent, and the fund with a target retirement date of 2015 lost 24.06 percent. Jane was devastated and flabbergasted. "I couldn't believe that these funds didn't do what they were advertised to do," she says. "I couldn't sleep."

When Jane called the mutual fund company (several times) for an explanation, the client service representatives she spoke with simply told her to stay the course. Jane, however, wanted answers. "How could a fund with a retirement date of 2010 lose 20 percent just two years before its maturity date?" she asks. "I want to know because I'm forced to postpone my retirement for at least two years as a result."

The retirement plan's role

Much of the growth in target-date funds is due to defined-contribution retirement plan assets invested in target-date strategies.

For the twelve months ended September 30, 2016, target-date funds took 18.4 percent of the $3.28 trillion total defined-contribution plan assets among the one thousand largest retirement plans, up from 16.8 percent in the prior period, according to *Pensions & Investments.*

All told, as of that date, target-date funds represented 17.7 percent of aggregate $1.96 trillion of assets among the top two hundred defined-contribution plans, up from 16.2 percent the year before.

These funds' potential for continued growth is so strong that Russell Investments predicts they could represent 70 percent of defined-contribution retirement plan assets in ten years.

That, in part, is because more and more defined-contribution retirement plans, such as 401(k) plans, are offering automatic enrollment. After the Pension Protection Act passed, target-date funds became eligible to be qualified default investment alternatives. Today, target-date funds are usually the default option when employers automatically enroll workers in 401(k) plans, and as of 2017, they can be found in nine out of ten workplace plans, according to Aon Hewitt. In other words, if you don't specify how you want your 401(k) plan assets invested, they will likely be invested in a target-date fund.

Here's another problem with target-date funds in retirement plans: The domination of the large 401(k) plan managers crowds out smaller (and possibly better) target-date funds. Think about it. If Vanguard manages your 401(k) plan, you're likely to be offered only Vanguard target-date funds, even if other target-date funds are better.

It's like going to Walmart and only being able to buy Walmart-brand paper towels.

The problem with target-date funds

You may think Jane's experience is a one-time incident. After all, target-date funds are very popular. Assets in target-date funds increased each year from 2008 to 2016. They hit a record $880 billion in 2016, up from $763 billion at the end of 2015, according to Morningstar. That's a lot of money, especially when you consider that the fund category didn't even exist until the mid-2000s. It took the entire mutual-fund industry more than fifty years to reach $2 trillion in assets.

Despite this popularity, however, Jane isn't alone in her experience. In 2008, Fidelity Freedom 2010 Fund and Vanguard Target Retirement 2010 Fund—some of the biggest names in the business—both lost more than 20 percent. I've heard worse though. Also in 2006, Fidelity Freedom Fund 2005—a fund targeting people who had already retired—lost 24 percent. I know the stock market plunged in 2008, but assets in a fund with a 2008 or 2010 target date should have been almost completely out of the stock market by then.

In fact, the markets hit an all-time high of fourteen thousand in October 2007, so why didn't the fund managers sell then? It seems obvious to me that a retirement fund with a target date of 2008 or 2010 should reduce its exposure to equities one to three years before the target date—especially if stocks reach an all-time high then.

In some cases, target-date funds are designed to stay significantly allocated to equities after the target retirement date, as I explain in "Understanding the glide path" below. But there are other explanations for what happened in 2008.

Understanding the glide path

Different mutual-fund companies take different approaches when their target-date funds reach their target dates. Some companies convert the assets into a retirement-income fund (either at the target year or later); others keep the assets in the original fund and keep the same name. For example, Vanguard Target Retirement 2010 is still around, even though 2010 has long since passed.

Either way, however, what happens to the fund's asset allocation when the target date is reached depends on its glide path. A glide path is simply the shift in a target-date fund's asset allocation over time.

There are two different approaches to glide paths. A two-retirement approach reduces the fund's equity exposure over time, reaching its most conservative point at the target date. A through-retirement approach also reduces the fund's equity exposure over time but does so through the target date, so the fund reaches its most conservative point years after the target date.

According to a recent research paper published by Morningstar, one of the key differences between target-date funds with two-retirement glide paths and target-date funds with through-retirement glide paths is the speed with which the allocation to stocks decreases. The average fund with a two-retirement glide path reaches its target retirement year with a 33 percent allocation to equities. Meanwhile, the average fund with a through-retirement glide path reaches its target retirement year with a 49 percent allocation to equities and then lowers its equity exposure over the next twenty to thirty years before reaching a final equity allocation of 28 percent.

The reason? Funds with through-retirement glide paths are designed to provide greater protection against longevity risk (since stocks tend to outperform other asset classes over time).

The problem? You could end up a few years into retirement with a significant allocation to equities.

Another explanation for what happened in 2008 that's bandied about is greed: holding more assets in stocks means more profit for the companies that manage target-date funds because actively managed stock funds generally charge higher expenses than bond funds.

Consider this as yet another explanation for what happened in 2008: The fund managers just didn't have the control you would expect them to have. That's because many target-date funds are simply comprised of other funds in the same fund family. For example, a Fidelity target-date fund invests in other Fidelity funds, just like a Vanguard target-date invests in other Vanguard funds. Want proof? According to Morningstar, the Vanguard target retirement 2015 fund has 99.99 percent of its client's money in other Vanguard funds as of April 30, 2017. Vanguard funds holding Vanguard funds and Fidelity funds holding Fidelity funds creates a possible conflict of interest.

Now, I'm not opposed to investing in funds of funds. In fact, the fund I manage does just that. However, there are two distinct differences between what I do and what large fund companies such as Vanguard and Fidelity do. First, I use mutual funds with which I have no business affiliation, meaning there is no conflict of interest. I select a fund strictly on the basis of my research strongly indicating that it is best for my shareholders. Second, I disclose the internal fees of the funds I buy called the internal holdings expense. Target-date funds aren't required to do that. So I have exposed a built-in conflict of interest and a layer of undisclosed fees built into target-date funds.

Target-date fund managers, not managing the underlying assets of their funds themselves, may not keep on top of the overall asset allocation.

Here's the proof. According to the Fidelity Freedom Fund 2005 prospectus dated May 30, 2009, the fund's principal investing strategy is "investing in a combination of underlying Fidelity equity, fixed-income, and short-term funds using a moderate asset-allocation strategy designed for investors expected to have retired around the year 2005."

The fund, the prospectus said, works by "allocating assets among underlying Fidelity Funds according to an asset-allocation strategy that becomes increasingly conservative until it reaches 20 percent in domestic equity funds, 35 percent in investment-grade fixed-income funds, 5 percent in high-yield fixed-income funds, and 40 percent in short-term funds (approximately ten to fifteen years after the year 2005)."

But according to Value Line Mutual Fund Analysis, Fidelity Freedom Fund 2005 had almost 40 percent in equities as of June 30, 2009. That's twice the amount suggested by the prospectus, a full four and a half years after the retirement date. The fund also had almost 8 percent of its assets invested in international equities, including the emerging markets. Looking through the prospectus, I couldn't find anything that explained how international equities could make up 8 percent of the fund.

You might think that mutual-fund companies changed after the debacle that was 2008. No to that too. According to BrightScope, a company that ranks 401(k) plans, from 2007 to 2010, the targeted percentage of stocks in target-date funds rose after the financial crisis from an average of 40 percent in 2007 to 43 percent in 2010. "Many fund companies failed to learn from the 2008 debacle, which failure will surely hurt participants again," BrightScope concluded.

Five years after I first wrote about this, in a speech made at the American Retirement Initiative's winter 2015 summit, then Securities and Exchange Commission (SEC) Commissioner Luis A. Aguilar expressed similar concerns with target-date funds. "Not only have target-date fund assets quadrupled since 2008, but their percentage of allocations to equities has also grown," he said. "Since 2005, many target-date funds have boosted their allocations to equities, both by extending their glide paths beyond the target date and by increasing equity allocations across the entire glide path. In and of itself, this may not be inappropriate as the greater exposure to equities may allow for greater returns. The issue, however, is whether investors appreciate the risks involved in having a greater allocation to equities, which generally are presumed riskier than fixed-income investments."

Who's the biggest offender?

According to Morningstar, some target-date fund providers have stable ratios of stocks to conservative investments over time while others (notably Fidelity, the market leader) have more fluctuations.

Separate research by Morningstar in 2013 found that thirteen of Fidelity's fourteen target-date funds performed worse than three-fourths of their competitors.

Also in 2013, the Center for Due Diligence, an independent information and strategic services firm serving retirement plan advisors, posted an analysis of Fidelity's target-date funds compared to similar offerings from the company's major competitors. When it came to funds with target retirement dates from 2010 to 2055, 79 percent of the Fidelity Freedom funds, 74 percent of the Fidelity Freedom K funds, and 68 percent of the Fidelity Advisor Freedom funds landed in the bottom half of category rankings.

Of course, stronger returns aren't everything. Phil Chiricotti, president of the Center for Due Diligence, said that Fidelity's more conservative glide path is one of the primary reasons its funds were underperforming, and a conservative glide path may be a good thing for risk-averse investors. But anecdotal evidence doesn't support that as I've explained with my discussion of what happened to some Fidelity target-date funds in 2008.

Well, you might say, that's just a problem with Fidelity. Other mutual-fund companies might do a better job. Nope—because there just aren't that many other mutual-fund companies heavily into the target-date fund business. According to an April 2013 report by the SEC's investor advisory committee, there is a high degree of saver concentration among just a few target-date funds. According to Morningstar, in 2016, three firms collectively held 71 percent of the market share in target-date funds: Vanguard (31.8 percent of market share), Fidelity (21.9 percent), and T. Rowe Price (16.8 percent). Seven firms held 88.3 percent. As a result, large numbers of investors, including individuals approaching retirement at the same time, will be affected by the approaches these companies adopt.

I saw this coming

I discussed the problem with target-date funds years ago. In February 2010, I wrote, "Do the funds live up to the hype? Let's see. To me, the biggest attraction these funds would have is if they did indeed proactively reallocate the portfolio to reduce the risk as you got within ten years of retirement and eliminated nearly all of it by five years out."

Target-date funds didn't do that then, and they don't do it now. The unfortunate thing is these funds are designed to appeal to investors such as Jane who just don't know any better. They're packaged as a turnkey approach to retirement, or, as Fidelity describes its Fidelity Freedom Funds, they're "all-in-one investment strategies that can help take the guesswork out of building and maintaining an age-based retirement portfolio." In other words, "It's easy! Just pick a fund with a date that matches your projected retirement, and we'll take care of the rest!" Sadly, many of these funds don't take care of the rest, and investors don't know it.

According to the aforementioned April 2013 SEC report, "Evidence suggests that individual investors are ill-equipped to identify those risk disparities among similar seeming funds. For example, on a survey commissioned by the SEC, only 36 percent of respondents (including 48 percent of target-date fund owners and 26 percent of nonowners) correctly answered a true-false question regarding whether target-date funds provide guaranteed income after retirement. Thirty percent (including 25 percent of owners and 34 percent of nonowners) answered incorrectly that target-date funds do provide guaranteed income. Fifteen percent of respondents said whether there is a guarantee depends on the fund and 20 percent said they didn't know."

Moreover, investors can't even rely on the professionals to help them with target-date funds because the professionals don't understand them either. According to the aforementioned April 2013 SEC report, many professional pension-fund consultants—those are the people who help select retirement plan fund options—underestimate the risk of target-date funds.

One unpublished study conducted for PIMCO in 2010 found that, although the average target-date fund exposed investors nearing retirement to a significantly higher maximum potential loss than most consultants surveyed deemed appropriate, only about 35 percent of those consultants viewed the glide paths as somewhat too highly inappropriate (i.e., too aggressive). "In other words, almost two-thirds of these pension consultants assumed that funds were invested more conservatively than was in fact the case," says the report.

"Bonds are terrible" (Warren Buffett, May 8, 2017)

Now, here's the really bad news about target-date funds (as if what I've written isn't bad enough): today's macroeconomic conditions are making the problem even worse.

Even if target-date funds work exactly as they're supposed to work—which I've already shown they don't—there's a problem given their heavy allocation to bonds.

What, you may ask? Aren't bonds supposed to be safer than stocks? In theory, yes; more bonds should make a fund safer because bonds tend to be less risky than stocks.

But that's not always the case. Don't take my word for it; consider the words of America's great stock market investor, Warren Buffett, who has made billions of dollars knowing where to invest his and his client's money, thanks in part to his uncanny ability to recognize trends before the masses do. In a televised interview on May 8, 2017, Buffett said, "Bonds are a terrible choice against stocks, and it's dictated by the mathematics. Thirty-year Treasury bonds are 3 percent now while stocks now trade for an average of about eighteen times forward earnings. Stocks offer growth while bonds offer fixed interest rates. Stocks are dirt cheap."

Right now, however, the bond market is near an all-time high as gauged by the low yield of the ten-year US Treasury. (Remember, bond prices and bond yields are inversely correlated. As the price goes up, the yield goes down.)

The first problem with the bond market today is that in moving assets from stocks to bonds as the retirement date approaches, a fund manager is forced to sell stocks and buy bonds, and those bonds are, simply explained, expensive. So by buying bonds at today's level, a portfolio manager is actually adding risk to a fund instead of reducing it, as you would expect in a target-date fund.

Additionally, should interest rates revert to their historic norms (which they will because they always have), bond prices will fall. The historic norm of the ten-year US Treasury yield is roughly 4 percent compared to 1.3759 percent, its all-time low reached in July 2016. And the increase in a bond's yield is always proportional to the decrease in a bond's price. If a ten-year bond yield increases by 1 percent, there would be a 5 percent drop in its price. So when the bond market normalizes, there could be a 10 percent to 15 percent drop in bond prices. This drop may be a fatal blow to retirees who've been thinking that as time marches on, their target-date funds will take on less risk.

These misunderstandings may be a ticking time bomb for the next generation of American retirees. T. Rowe Price, for example, uses a 90 percent stock and 10 percent bond allocation for investors thirty years from retirement but a 20 percent stock and 80 percent bond mix thirty years after the retirement date. That's a lot of bonds!

Again, five years after I first wrote about this, in his speech made at the American Retirement Initiative's winter 2015 summit, Aguilar expressed similar concerns with target-date funds. "The belief is that an improving economy will eventually force the Federal Reserve to raise interest rates and that this may cause another 'taper tantrum,' in which bond prices plummet," he said, adding that this possibility raises a number of questions for target-date fund providers.

How do we warn investors about this potential market disruption?

What are these funds doing to prepare for another possible taper tantrum? Are they diversifying into other assets besides bonds?

If so, does this present new risks that should be disclosed to investors?

These are all good questions if I do say so myself (as I have).

The watchful eye of the SEC

The good news, if there is any, is that the SEC got wind of this problem, and 2010 proposed a rule that, if adopted, would require any target-date fund that includes the target date in its name to disclose its allocation at the projected retirement date "immediately adjacent to" the first use of the fund's name in marketing materials. The rule would also require more disclosure about a fund's asset allocation and glide path. The SEC invited comments from the public, but for whatever reason, nothing came of this review in 2010.

Then in 2013, the SEC's investor advisory committee adopted recommendations, asking the agency to rewrite its proposed rule on target-date retirement funds. The recommendations would expand the 2010 SEC proposal with five recommendations. Mutual fund companies, the committee said, should develop a glide path illustration for target-date funds based on risk rather than asset allocation alone; adopt a standard methodology to be used in the risk-based and asset-allocation glide path illustrations; clearly explain the assumptions used to design and manage the fund to attain the target risk level over the life of the fund; warn that target-date fund returns are not guaranteed and that losses are possible, including at or after the target date; and amend fee disclosure requirements to show the impact of those costs over the lifetime of the investment.

"In making this change in disclosure, we are actually going to teach investors something really important that most of them don't understand," said James Glassman, a committee member and founding executive director of the George W. Bush Institute, at a hearing. "There is more to risk than asset allocation."

I thought that was a good sign that something (finally!) would be done about target-date funds. Investors needed to be informed that these funds have better marketing strategies than investment strategies.

I was even more hopeful when in 2014, the SEC reopened its 2010 proposed rule for public comment in 2014.

But guess what? We're still waiting for a final rule.

And if you think government always works that slowly, consider this. In the spring of 2013, it took the SEC only weeks to declare that public companies could announce vital information via social media. Let's hope that they move as fast on a matter that affects most Americans' 401(k) accounts.

Change on the horizon?

That said, in his speech at the American Retirement Initiative's winter 2015 summit, Aguilar did express concerns with target-date funds.

"These funds are particularly attractive to investors who are not financially experienced," he said. "Evidence suggests that investors may perceive these funds to be virtually risk free... Target date funds, however, do not contain guarantees. Investors in these funds are not assured they will have sufficient retirement income at the target date, and there is no guarantee that investors will not lose some, or even all, of their investment."

According to Aguilar, the experience of target-date fund investors during the financial crisis should have been a wake-up call that these funds were not performing as advertised; he criticized the fact that no rules about disclosures have been passed since then. He points out that the need for the SEC to act "has taken on an added urgency in recent years as investors have continued to invest in target-date funds in record numbers."

"The SEC staff should move quickly to advise the Commission on how best to move forward to help individual investors and plan providers," he said. "It is imperative that investors better understand the risks presented by target-date funds."

Aguilar also suggested that the SEC dust off its 2010 target-date fund proposal and consider what actions may be appropriate, in light of all the evidence gathered.

"The consequences of investors continuing to be ill-informed about the inherent risks of target-date funds are simply too grave," he said.

This is the latest alert from the SEC regarding Target Retirement funds:

> Risk Alert
> Office of Compliance Inspections and Examinations
> November 7, 2019
> Top Compliance Topics Observed in Examinations of Investment Companies and Observations from Money Market Fund and Target Date Fund Initiatives

I. Introduction

The Office of Compliance Inspections and Examinations ("OCIE") is issuing this Risk Alert to provide investment companies, investors, and other market participants with information on the most often cited deficiencies and weaknesses that the staff has observed in recent examinations of registered investment companies ("funds"). In addition, this Risk Alert includes observations by the staff from national examination initiatives focusing on money-market funds and target-date funds.

TDF Initiative: OCIE staff examined over-thirty TDFs, including both "to" and "through" funds, to review whether the TDF's assets were invested according to the asset allocations stated in the funds' prospectuses and whether the associated investment risks were consistent with fund disclosures (including representations made in marketing materials).

OFIE staff observed that most TDFs appeared to be in general compliance with the 1940 Act in the areas reviewed; however, instances of deficiencies or weaknesses related to TDFs' disclosures and compliance programs were noted. For example:

- *Some TDFs had incomplete and potentially misleading disclosures in their prospectuses and advertisements, including disclosures regarding:*
    - Asset allocations, both current and prospective over time. For example, the TDFs had marketing materials with asset allocation disclosures that differed from the TDF's prospectus disclosures.
    - Glide path changes and the impact of these glide path changes on asset allocations.

- ○ Conflicts of interest, such as those that may result from the use of affiliated funds and affiliated investment advisers.
- *Many TDFs had incomplete or missing policies and procedures, including those for:*
  - ○ Monitoring asset allocations, including ongoing monitoring.
  - ○ Overseeing implementation of changes to their current glide path asset allocations.
  - ○ Overseeing advertisements and sales literature, which resulted in advertising disclosures that were inconsistent with prospectus disclosures and were potentially misleading. ○ Monitoring whether disclosures regarding glide path deviations were accurate.

IV. Conclusion

In sharing the information in this Risk Alert, OCIE encourages funds to review their practices, policies, and procedures in these areas and to consider improvements in funds' compliance programs, as may be appropriate.

*****

I've explained what's wrong with target-date funds; now I'd like to show you some examples focusing on these three 2020 target-date funds, which, as noted, are designed for individuals retiring in or very close to the year 2020.

Many such funds simply aren't living up to expectations and are failing to protect the soon-to-be retirees who invest in them from big market losses. If anything should be clear from this chapter, it's that target-date funds can't protect you from losses. They didn't in 2008, they didn't in 2018, and they won't in the future.

Fidelity Freedom 2020 Fund (FFFDX)

Designed for investors who anticipate retiring in or within a few years of the fund's target retirement year, this fund "seeks high total return until its target retirement date. Thereafter, the fund seeks high current income first and capital appreciation second."

The fund seeks to achieve this goal by allocating assets among underlying Fidelity funds according to a "neutral" asset-allocation strategy that adjusts over time until it reaches an allocation similar to that of the Freedom Income Fund.

Where does the fund stand now, a year after its target date? As of June 30, 2021, the fund's composition was 23.04 percent domestic equities, 26.23 percent international equities, 37.40 percent bonds, and the balance short-term debt (such as money market funds and US Treasuries).

In theory, that might seem reasonable. You need equities for growth as you approach retirement. And the fund has delivered growth over the longer term. As of June 30, 2021, its ten-year average annual return was a solid 7.83 percent.

But you want to cut your risk exposure back as you near retirement to minimize the effects of market volatility. You can tolerate such swings when you have years to ride them out, but when you need to withdraw your money, those swings become problematic. Is FFFDX's 49 percent total equity allocation reasonable a year after your retirement date?

During the beginning of the COVID-19 pandemic (from February 19, 2020, to March 23, 2020), the fund lost 19.69 percent. That's a big hit for folks that were already a year into retirement.

Yes, I am aware that the markets have bounced back since then. But that isn't my point. The problem is the billions of dollars that the retirees pulled out after the huge decline that didn't experience the recovery. If the fund has held better-diversified equity positions, the drop would have been greatly decreased, and maybe thousands more shareholders would have enjoyed the bounce back.

In 2018, FFFDX was down 5.20 percent, more than the S&P 500 Index (down 4.38 percent), the Fidelity Freedom 2020

Composite Index (down 3.75 percent), and the Morningstar Target-Date 2020 category (down 4.49 percent), all of which it shows as benchmarks. So not only was FFFDX losing money for retirees invested in it a year before needed that money; it was losing money faster than all of its benchmarks, even one operated by Fidelity itself! Ow-pha!

Now skeptics might note that FFFDX has only been down in three of the past ten calendar years. I understand that point. But to be down so much a year before the target date tells me something is wrong.

It's also worth noting that FFFDX has $26.2 billion in assets as of the end of 2018. That's a lot of shareholder accounts.

Vanguard Target Retirement 2020 Fund (VTWNX)

Like FFFDX, VTWNX has considerable assets under management: $31.7 billion.

Also designed for investors who anticipate retiring in or within a few years of the fund's target retirement year (2018 to 2022, according to Vanguard), VTWNX invests in five Vanguard index funds, holding approximately 47 percent of assets in stocks and 53 percent in bonds as of June 30, 2021.

Its objective is to provide broad diversification while incrementally decreasing exposure to stocks and increasing exposure to bonds as each fund's target retirement date approaches. It continues to adjust for approximately seven years after its target date until its allocations match that of the Target Retirement Income Fund. So in 2027, it should be a bond fund.

Not surprisingly, the fund lost money in 2018, just as FFFDX did. In 2018, VTWNX was down 4.24 percent, more than the S&P 500 Index (again, down 4.38 percent) and its benchmark Target Retirement 2020 Composite Index (down 4.13 percent). During the first quarter sell-off, this fund lost 19.37 percent and billions of dollars were pulled out—dollars that didn't participate in the recovery.

Interesting for a fund that shows its risk potential being a three on a scale of one to five. If you're preparing to retire and have amassed, say a $1,000,000 portfolio, how do you feel about your nest egg being down more than $40,000 this year?

T. Rowe Price Retirement 2020 Fund (TRRBX)

Let's look at one more example, TRRBX, which, like other target-date funds, invests in a diversified portfolio of other T. Rowe Price stock and bond funds. It has $18.4 billion in assets under management.

T. Rowe Price offers more detail on its website than many other mutual fund marketers, indicating that as the fund nears its target retirement date, its allocation between T. Rowe Price stock and bond funds will become more conservative based on a predetermined glide path.

But the website notes that "the allocations shown in the glide path are referred to as 'neutral' allocations because they do not reflect the tactical decisions made by T. Rowe Price to overweight or underweight a particular asset class or sector based on its market outlook."

T. Rowe Price makes its holding harder to find than the other funds I've mentioned. It says 97.8 percent of its assets are allocated to "other" as of November 30, 2018. (How's that for transparency?) Digging a little deeper and looking at its top ten holdings though, six are stock funds.

But that shouldn't matter, since TRRBX's managers can reallocate based on what portfolio managers think is best given current market conditions, right? Does that mean the fund should have performed better than other target-date funds that struggled in 2018 because surely, its managers reallocated as the market took a dive?

Nope. As of December 31, 2018, the fund's handy risk-potential chart shows its risk as somewhere between "moderate" and "higher," meaning portfolio managers haven't reallocated. In 2018, the fund was down 4.94 percent, more than its benchmarks: the S&P Target Date 2020 Index (down 4.16 percent) and the Lipper Mixed-Asset Target 2020 Funds Average (down 4.59 percent).

During the first quarter sell-off, this fund lost 23.90 percent and billions of dollars were pulled out—dollars that didn't participate in the recovery. The June 30, 2021 allocation was 50.46 percent stocks and 49.54 percent bonds.

The return of the bear

What happened in 2018? Santa left a lump of coal in most investors' stockings in 2018. The market shuddered, and it was bad. On December 24, the S&P 500 Index fell into bear-market territory (a loss of 20 percent from its high) in post-market trading.

That was the worst Christmas Eve trading session ever and the first time the index had entered a bear market since 2009. And it happened quickly: In just ten calendar days, the index fell about 250 points, close to 10 percent.

The S&P 500 Index wasn't alone. Other indices—the Nasdaq Composite Index and Russell 2000 Index—had already entered bear markets.

This provided a harsh reminder to target-date-fund investors that broad diversification doesn't ensure they won't experience difficult losses—and perhaps harkened back to 2008 when target-date investors on the verge of retirement experienced hefty losses.

Learning from the past

When you're a target-date investor and market volatility gets you and your portfolio down, you're in a tough spot. Some target-date investors have many years to make up ground before they retire and start withdrawing assets, but many others hope to retire soon. They have only two choices: work longer to make up the losses or simply learn to live with less in retirement. Neither is likely appealing.

But that's what happened in 2008. Target-date funds with retirement dates beyond 2020 experienced losses exceeding 30 percent. But investors in those funds had years to continue saving, and they were able to take advantage of the bull market that started in March 2009. Investors in nearer-dated funds, including those set to retire in 2010, weren't so fortunate.

Consider those unlucky enough to be allocated to the Oppenheimer Transition 2010 Fund, which had around 70 percent of its assets allocated to equities just two years before it reached its target date, according to Morningstar. It experienced a 41 percent loss in 2008. Investors just couldn't recover from that. How could you?

And 2008 unearthed another risk: fixed income. Widely considered a safe haven, it turned out bonds weren't what they appeared to be either. Some target-date funds had aggressively allocated their fixed-income component to risky high-yield bond funds, which can move in the same direction as equities.

Did portfolio managers learn from the past?

No, but don't take my word for it. "What managers generally have not done is reduce their overall equity exposure," says a September 2018 CNBC article, "These 401(k) Funds *took a beating in 2008—and it could happen again.* If anything, they've added more stock exposure for investors who are in the middle of their careers."

"This way, these savers can continue to capture market gains and stave off the risk they will outlive their savings in retirement," said Jeff Holt, director, multi-asset and alternative strategies at Morningstar, quoted in the CNBC article. "Target-date funds aren't fundamentally different in how they are built now versus 2008. They still hold a significant amount of equities at the retirement date."

If anything, 2018 made the point that target-date funds haven't changed loud and clear. Before December 2018, we'd been in the midst of a historically significant bull market since the last bear market ended in March 2009. That's almost ten-year of bull market, which is virtually unprecedented. Anyone with any sense knew we would undoubtedly experience a market correction at some point—but target-date fund managers didn't seem to care. They just rode the highs, basking in the glow of positive performance, until they couldn't.

The assets under management of the three funds as of June 30, 2021, I reviewed, are notable: FFFDX has $26.2 billion, VTWNX has $31.7 billion, and TRRBX has $18.4 billion. That's a total of $76.3 billion in shareholder accounts.

How much is $76.3 billion? Well, if you had it, you could give every man, woman, and child in the United States $234. You could give every retiree in the United States (an estimated population of around 50 million) $1,526, or you could be selfish and keep it to yourself, in which case you'd have to spend $4,180,822 a day for the next fifty years to deplete your stash (and that's assuming you stuff it under your mattress without any interest compounding!).

The point is, it's a lot of money to have sitting around in target-date funds—and the 5 percent of it lost by portfolio managers in 2018 is close to $4 billion. That's even more money to lose on behalf of trusting retirees.

What can you do?

We've established that target-date funds are riskier investments than they're widely considered and that the SEC isn't acting promptly to correct those misperceptions. That being the case, what can you do?

It's simple: don't invest in target-date funds—ever.

It just doesn't make sense. Putting each one of the same age into the same asset allocation defeats the purpose of financial planning, which is supposed to construct a portfolio appropriate to an individual investor's investment goals and risk tolerance and change it over time based on changes in that an individual investor's circumstances. Target-date funds are like a doctor writing every fifty-year-old a prescription for blood pressure medication because that's what all fifty-year-olds need, and then switching the prescription to cholesterol-lowering medication in five years because that's what all fifty-five-year-olds need.

Remember Jane, whose target-date retirement fund lost 20.67 percent just two years before its maturity date? She gets it. "I've always been told if something seems too good to be true, it probably is, and these funds were that," she says. "Somebody was sleeping at the wheel, and I hope what you're writing helps avoid another person making the same mistake that I did. People have to understand that these funds have disappointed in the past and will most likely disappoint in the future."

So there you have it. I showed you that inside your 401(k) lies another set of lies designed to keep you from achieving a retirement free from income tax and true investment diversification.

I'm bringing sector back—sector investing!

Chapter 9

How to Invest in a *Gig* Retirement Plan

In more than thirty years, I've never heard the Fed make such a bullish statement, in any amount necessary. If that's not a buy sign, then a buy sign does not exist.

—Mark Anthony Grimaldi, March 25, 2020

My investing approach involves sector rotation, which is the movement of money from stocks of one industry to stocks of another in anticipation or response to the changing stages of the economic cycle. The economy moves in reasonably predictable cycles, and you can take advantage of it. Here's how.

What are sectors?

First, let's look at what sectors are. Standard & Poor's (S&P) and Morgan Stanley Capital International (MSCI) created a method of sorting publicly traded companies based on their primary business activity. These are called sectors and industries and are together referred to as the Global Industry Classification Standard (GICS). There are eleven sectors and twenty-four industry groups. Below I listed the sectors because that's what I focus on in my investing strategy.

1. *Information technology (IT).* The IT sector consists of companies that develop or distribute technological items or services, including computers, microprocessors, and operating systems, as well as internet-related services.

   Examples of companies in this sector include well-known names like Microsoft, Apple, and Amazon. (Yes, Amazon is a retailer, but it's an internet retailer. It is a multinational technology company that also focused on cloud computing, digital streaming, and artificial intelligence. Thus, it's in the IT sector.)

   Many believe that such a lopsided market isn't healthy. Regardless, IT is always a sector to watch, having undergone massive changes over the past two decades due to the rapid rise in technology-based companies.

   You probably recall the technology bubble (more specifically, the dot-com bubble) two decades ago. This rapid rise in US technology stock valuations was fueled by investments in internet companies in the late 1990s. The mania drove the value of equity markets up with the Nasdaq Composite Index rising from under one thousand in 1995 to more than five thousand in 2000.

   The crash was equally spectacular, bringing home the point: different sectors perform differently at different times. That's smart investor rotates sectors when investing.
2. *Health care.* The healthcare sectors consist of pharmaceutical companies, medical supply companies, and other products or services that seek to improve the human body or mind.

   Companies in this sector that may come to mind quickly include Pfizer and Johnson & Johnson, thanks to COVID-19 vaccines. Other examples of healthcare companies are United Health, CVS, McKesson, and Siemens, which provide medical care, drugs, and devices.

   Cannabis companies are a new but rapidly growing part of the healthcare sector. Currently, the more well-known ones include Canopy Growth and Aurora Cannabis with market caps of $7.8 billion and $1.4 billion respectively in June 2021.

3. *Financials.* The financial sector consists of companies involved in finance, investing, and the movement or storage of money—banks, credit card issuers, asset managers, credit unions, insurance companies, and mortgage real estate investment trusts (REITs).

   Companies in this sector include Bank of America, JPMorgan Chase, and Goldman Sachs (all banks), as well as Berkshire Hathaway, American Express, and Aon.

   The financial sector is one of the largest portions of the S&P 500 Index, and companies within this sector are usually relatively stable, as many are well established.

4. *Consumer Discretionary.* Consumer discretionary products are luxuries—i.e., the items or services you use that are necessary for survival. Think cars, jewelry, sporting goods, and electronic devices for products, and include vacations, hotels, and dining in restaurants for services.

   The demand for consumer discretionary products and services depends on individual wealth, which in turn depends on economic conditions. So they tend to perform well when the economy performs well.

   Most companies in this sector are easily recognized. Some examples include Starbucks, Best Buy, Home Depot, McDonald's, and Nike. McDonald's may not sound like a luxury, but that's how S&P sees it.

5. *Communication services.* The communication services sector consists of companies that keep people connected—phone plan providers, internet providers, and includes media and entertainment companies.

   Some old-school names in the sector are AT&T and Verizon. The more exciting part of the sector includes companies like CBS and Walt Disney. In fact, the top ten holdings in the sector include three of the four so-called FAANG stocks: Facebook, Netflix, and Google parent

Alphabet. (Amazon is the other, which, as noted above, is considered an IT stock.)

Communications services is a fairly new sector launched in 2018 to replace telecommunications. That change reflected an evolving world. The new communications services sector retained traditional telecom stocks like AT&T and Verizon but now includes media companies like the ones mentioned above, as well as social media names like Twitter and Facebook.

6. *Industrials.* Industrials don't sound like an exciting sector—factories and smokestacks likely come to find. But the sector actually includes a wide range of companies that manufacture and distribute capital goods in support of varying industries.

   These industries include construction, engineering, aerospace, defense, and more. Everything from airlines and railroad companies to military weapons manufacturers are industrial stocks. Since the range of companies is so large, the sector has fourteen different industries.

   Stocks in this sector include Delta Air Lines, Southwest Airlines, FedEx, Boeing, General Electric, 3M, and Honeywell.

   Industrials stocks tend to thrive in economic recoveries, like the one from the COVID-19 pandemic. When you think about it, that makes sense: people travel and buy goods (which factories need to make) when economies are doing well.

7. *Consumer staples.* Consumer staples companies consist of those that provide the necessities of life—think food and beverages, household products, and personal products (like soaps and razors).

   Consumer staples companies are generally well known because people see their products in stores regularly. Examples are Procter & Gamble (which produces laundry detergent under brand names such as Dawn and Tide), Coca-Cola, General Mills, and Kroger.

Most consumer staples stocks are noncyclical, meaning they perform the same at different stages of the economic cycle. That's because they produce or sell goods or services that are always in demand. Investors often like them for their low volatility.

8. *Energy.* The energy sector consists of companies that play a part in the oil, gas, and consumable fuels business—finding, drilling, and extracting, and refining.

   Examples include Exxon Mobil and Chevron, which extract and refine gas, and Kinder Morgan, which transports fuel to gas stations. Not all of these names are well known.

   The energy sector is usually considered cyclical (or sensitive to the economic cycle). Additionally, seasons play a critical role in the sector's performance, increasing demand for gasoline in the summer and a decrease in demand during the winter. According to State Street, however, energy did not make the top or bottom three sectors during any recent business cycle, suggesting it is not as sensitive to economic cycles as many people think.

9. *Utilities.* The utilities sector consists of companies involved in power generation and distribution and infrastructure development and operations. In layman's terms, utility companies provide or generate electricity, water, and gas to buildings and households, or play some role in doing so (like sanitation and waste disposal).

   While this may sound dull, there is one exciting part of this sector: Many utility companies are developing renewable energy sources, such as solar and wind. So green energy companies are utilities. Examples include Duke Energy, Southern Company, and Edison.

   Utilities aren't considered cyclical stocks because people always need power. But power demand does rise as the economy rebounds (as we saw as people emerged from COVID-19 lockdowns), so let's there is a cyclical element to this sector.

10. *Real Estate.* Real estate, which became a sector fairly recently in 2015, includes realtors, property managers, and real estate investment trusts (REITs).

    You may not recognize the names: Companies in the sector include American Tower, Boston Properties, and Equinix.

    Real estate is considered a cyclical industry because it is impacted by economic cycles and also because demand has historically outweighed supply.

11. *Materials.* Companies within the materials sector are involved in the discovery, development, and processing of raw materials. In other words, they provide the stuff needed for other sectors to function. Think make basic products like plastic, lumber, chemicals, paint, and glue.

    Obvious examples are mining and forestry companies. But companies that are not typically associated with materials but are nevertheless in the sector include container and packaging companies, such as the Intertape Polymer, which manufactures tape.

    Materials companies tend to be cyclical. For example, between May of 2008 and February of 2009, during the so-called Global Financial Crisis, the sector's value fell by more than 55 percent.

Why sectors matter

It's simple: in the history of the United States, a sector has never become worthless.

Yes, sectors evolve, but they never disappear. Fifty years ago, electric cars were in the transportation sector? No, but they are now. How would you like to be the person who sold all your GM shares in 2007 (pre-bankruptcy) and invested that money in Tesla as it started its ascent? If you held a position in the transportation sector, that's exactly what you did.

That's because sectors are always self-correcting. If in March 2020 you wanted to hold a position in the pharmaceutical company that developed the COVID-19 vaccine, you could have purchased shares of all the drug companies that you felt would be the first to market, but this approach wouldn't ensure you held the winning company. You could have purchased a no-load mutual fund that invests in the healthcare sector. If the company that invented the vaccine wasn't in the sector, it still would have moved with the release of a vaccine. Yes, your exposure to the winning company could be diluted by the other segments of the sector, but that "dilution risk" pales in comparison to the "capital risk" of holding dozens of companies whose vaccines never were bought to the market.

Sectors can drive the performance of the S&P 500 Index. In fact, as of June 2021, the combined market valuation of just five stocks, most in the communications services sector—Apple, Microsoft, Amazon, Alphabet (Google), and Facebook—represent more than 20 percent of the total of all companies in the S&P 500 Index. When they go up, the index goes up; when they go down, the index goes down.

Sector Weights (as of December 2020)

S&P 500 Index Sectors	Sector Weight
Information Technology	27.6%
Health Care	13.5%
Consumer Discretionary	12.7%
Communication Services	10.8%
Financials	10.4%
Industrials	8.4%
Consumer Staples	6.5%
Utilities	2.8%
Materials	2.6%
Real Estate	2.4%
Energy	2.3%

Sector breakdowns also help investors determine the allocation of funds within a portfolio. Broadly speaking, if an investor wants to create a diversified portfolio, the portfolio should include stocks from a variety of sectors. However, some investors want exposure to only certain sectors, like technology or energy. In this case, they can confine their investing to only the sectors they are interested in.

Are there ever sectors added to the economy? Yes, but at present, there are eleven core sectors, and that number hasn't changed in a long time.

Do sectors become irrelevant to the economy and thus fade away? No. As the economy evolves, so do the sectors.

Do individual companies evolve like sectors? Some do. Amazon started out selling books and grew into the largest online retailer in the world. Apple helped launch the personal computer, then built on that technology to produce the iPod and iPhone. But those are the rare exceptions (and by the way, both were pulled into more appropriate sectors as they evolved and gained more economic relevance).

But wait. There's another danger to investing in individual companies. They fail. In a typical year, there are around 750 initial public offerings (IPOs) listed on stock exchanges. One might assume there are well over 50,000 publicly traded companies on US exchanges then. In fact, there are only approximately 3,500 publicly traded companies on US exchanges. Believe it or not, hundreds usually get delisted every month. There are three main reasons: they get acquired, they do not trade actively enough (sometimes called illiquidity), and they file for bankruptcy. Is it accurate to say hundreds of listed companies go bankrupt every year? No. That's because *hundreds* go bankrupt every year. If you want to steer clear of that risk, I suggest investing in sectors.

Yes, I bring sector back! (Sorry, Justin Timberlake. I couldn't resist.)

Part 4

Taxes, Distributions, and Inheritance

Chapter 10

Taxation of the Gig Retirement Plan

Why aren't you signed up for the 401K? I'd never be able to run that far.

—Scott Adams, Dilbert, May 2, 2001

The tax code is like a Rubik's Cube. Once you know the secret, it can be solved in seconds.

—Mark Anthony Grimaldi

Tax fact: the income tax rate is among the *highest* in the IRS code.

Tax fact: the capital gain tax rate is among the *lowest* in IRS code.

Tax fact: 401(k)s/IRAs *convert* all capital gains to income at tax time!

Tax fact: A gig RetireSmart plan can tell the difference between income and capital gains. So at tax time, you don't pay a penny more in taxes than you should. In this chapter, I'll walk you through some basics you'll need to know as you plan how to invest in a gig retirement plan.

The IRS—now onto gig workers

Once upon a time, the gig workers were the exception rather than the rule; today, the IRS has an entire section of its website dedicated to gig workers. Before we talk about the taxation of the gig retirement plan then, let's review some of the tax basics you need to know as a gig worker.

The IRS recognizes several kinds of gig workers, but many of you reading this (and the ones who need help) are likely self-employed. Generally, you are considered self-employed if you do business as a sole proprietor or an independent contractor, you're a member of a partnership that does business, or you're otherwise in business for yourself (including a part-time business).

Before you start the tax process, be sure your business is indeed a business. Some (okay, many) people have tried to claim deductions for what is not a business but a hobby. Thc IRS has detailed instructions for determining which yours is, but in brief, the key feature of a business is that people do it to make a profit. The IRS lists out nine characteristics of such an endeavor, including whether you carry on the activity in a businesslike manner and maintain complete and accurate books and records; whether you depend on income from the activity for your livelihood; and whether you or your advisors have the knowledge needed to carry on the activity as a successful business.

Let's look at this one in more detail though, whether you carry on the activity in a businesslike manner and maintain complete and accurate books and records. If your business is going to be a business from a tax perspective, it needs to be separate from your personal finances. So if you are going down the route of the gig worker, the first thing you must do is get an employer identification number (EIN), which is also called federal tax identification number. It's like a Social Security number, but it's used to identify a business entity. Why do you want one? To keep your business income separate from your personal income, from an IRS perspective. Many websites will try to sell you EIN services, but don't fall for it. You can get an EIN free from the IRS website (usually, instantly).

Next, you'll need to keep track of your income and expenses and file an annual income tax return (likely, a different tax form submitted with your regular tax form). Each April, you will submit that form listing your income and deductions (the expenses you had in the course of doing business).

But that's not your only responsibility. During the course of the year, you will also likely need to pay estimated taxes. An employee of a company usually has his or her income tax withheld from his or her paycheck. If that doesn't happen because you work for yourself, you will have to do it yourself by writing a check to the IRS. You generally have to make estimated tax payments if you expect to owe tax of $1,000 or more when your annual return is filed, and you make those payments quarterly. The amount is what you expect to owe in taxes on the income you generate. The IRA website can help you calculate that, but it's often the job of an accountant.

I don't want to go into too much detail about how you pay taxes on a quarter-to-quarter or year-to-year basis because this isn't an accounting book, and you can easily get that information from the IRS website. What I do want to discuss is what you need to know about taxes as you plan how to invest in a gig retirement plan.

First up, the different kinds of income.

Earned income and capital gains—the ins and outs of taxation

"Our new Constitution is now established and has an appearance that promises permanency; but in this world, nothing can be said to be certain, except death and taxes," wrote Benjamin Franklin in 1789 in a letter to Jean-Baptiste Leroy.

While true, Franklin could hardly have anticipated the complication of today's tax code, which is 74,608 pages long. That is 187 times longer than it was a century ago, according to Wolters Kluwer, CCH, which has taken on the less-than-exciting task of analyzing the tax code since 1913.

Let's try to make the subject simple by breaking it down into two parts: ordinary income taxes and capital gains taxes. For fun, I'll also throw in some information about 401(k) plans, the (allegedly) great savior of Americans' retirement.

Ordinary people, ordinary income

Ordinary income is simple to define. It is the income you earn by providing services or selling goods. So it would include your wages (whether you are employed by a company or self-employed), bonuses, commissions, interest, rent, royalties, and the like. For a business, it would include profits earned from selling goods or services. Let's look at two examples, one for a private individual and one for a business.

Individual. Let's say you earn $50,000 per year working for a major retailer. If you have no other source of income, you will report $50,000 of gross income on your year-end tax return. If you also receive $2,000 in rental income from a property you lease, you would report an additional $24,000 a year in gross income, for a total of $74,000.

Business. Let's say you sell $200,000 worth of goods in a year, but your total operating expenses are $125,000. You would report the difference, $75,000, as a profit.

How ordinary income is taxed

Ordinary income is taxed at different rates. It depends on the amount of income received from a given taxpayer in a given tax year. Single filers pay different rates than married filers, for example. And those who earn more pay a higher percentage of their income.

Tax rates range from 10 percent to 37 percent in 2022, but calculating them is not as simple as multiplying your income by a given tax rate. That's because tax rates are so-called marginal rates. For example, if you're a single filer with $32,000 in taxable income, you're in the 12 percent tax bracket in 2022. But you don't pay 12 percent on $32,000; you pay only 10 percent on the first $9,275 and 12 percent on the rest. Sound complicated? The folks at the Tax

Foundation were kind enough to simplify it for us as the tables below illustrate.

Note that your personal income tax can also be offset with deductions. They essentially reduce your income for tax purposes. The result is what is called your adjusted income. You can take a standard deduction—in 2022, it is $12,950 if you file as a single person, $25,900 if you and your spouse file jointly, and $18,800 if you file as head of household. You can also itemize your deductions if you think they will add up to more than the standard deduction.

Married Tax Brackets (2022)

Marginal Rate	Income Range	Taxes You Pay
10%	$0 to $20,550	10% of taxable income
12%	$20,550 to $83,550	$1,990 plus 12% of the amount over $19,900
22%	$83,550 to $178,150	$9,328 plus 22% of the amount over $81,050
24%	$178,150 to $340,100	$29,502 plus 24% of the amount over $172,750
32%	$340,100 to $431,900	$67,206 plus 32% of the amount over $329,850
35%	$431,900 to $647,850	$95,686 plus 35% of the amount over $418,850
37%	$647,850 or more	$168,993.50 plus 37% of the amount over $628,300

Single Tax Brackets (2022)

Marginal Rate	Income Range	Taxes You Pay
10%	$0 to $10,275	10% of taxable income
12%	$10,275 to $41,775	$995 plus 12% of the amount over $9,950

22%	$41,775 to $88,075	$4,664 plus 22% of the amount over $40,525
24%	$88,075 to $170,050	$14,751 plus 24% of the amount over $86,375
32%	$170,050 to $215,950	$33,603 plus 32% of the amount over $164,925
35%	$215,950 to $539,900	$47,843 plus 35% of the amount over $209,425
37%	$539,900 or more	$157,804.25 plus 37% of the amount over $523,600

Beware the AMT!

Then there is the dreaded alternative minimum tax (AMT). The AMT is a parallel tax system that requires high-income taxpayers to calculate their tax bill twice—once under the ordinary income tax system then again under the AMT. The taxpayer then pays the higher of the two. This controversial system was created in the 1960s to prevent high-income taxpayers from avoiding taxes. But AMT is a complication best left to professionals.

Reducing ordinary income with a 401(k) plan—a fool's errand

Now that we know what ordinary income is and how it is taxed, let's add the 401(k) plan to our discussion. Can't income tax be reduced by contributing to a 401(k) plan?

A 401(k) plan is a retirement-savings vehicle funded by your wages. Your employer may match part of your contributions, but even this match is considered additional wages.

Because you are not taxed on wages that go in the 401(k) plan, you are taxed when you withdraw money from your 401(k) plan. The way the IRS views it, wages go in and wages come out. So you may not be paying income taxes on the wages you contribute to a 401(k) plan, but you do pay income taxes on wages you withdraw.

And you pay them on both the federal and state level, most likely (unless you're lucky enough to live in a state with no income taxes).

And therein lies the problem. No matter how you invest, all the money in your 401(k) plan will eventually be taxed as income—and other than the federal estate tax, the income tax is the highest you can pay.

401(k) lies exposed

In my first book, *The Money Compass*, the chapter that got the most attention was the one on 401(k) plans. My readers couldn't believe their 401(k) plans were their biggest tax generators for Uncle Sam. But it's true.

Lie 1: a 401(k) will keep your income taxes low.
Truth: a 401(k) doesn't lower income taxes—it simply defers them to retirement when you can least afford to pay them.
Lie 2: your beneficiary can inherit your 401(k) tax efficiently.
Truth: your beneficiary will pay every penny in taxes that you would have paid.
Lie 3: a 401(k) will keep your income taxes low.
Truth: a 401(k) converts a low- or no-tax event to a high tax event.

The system is designed—or rigged, if you want to call it that—to trap you into a loop of never-ending taxes. As I've said during my TV interviews, "The rich pass laws to make the middle class subsidize the poor." This is just one of the reasons we are witnessing the destruction of the middle class.

Capital gains (and losses)

Capital gains are profits realized from the sale of a capital asset. Common capital assets are businesses, real estate, works of art, and investments. But according to the IRS, "almost everything you own and use for personal or investment purposes is a capital asset," including "personal-use items like household furnishings."

Sometimes when you sell an asset, you receive more for it than you originally paid for it. In this case, you have a capital gain. So if you buy a used car today for $10,000 and sell it tomorrow for $15,000, you have a $5,000 capital gain. Similarly, if you buy a stock today for $50 per share and sell it next week for $100 per share, you have a $50-per-share capital gain.

Of course, we always don't make such wise decisions. If you are unfortunate enough to receive less for a capital asset than you paid for, you experience a capital loss. Consider the car example above.

If you buy a used car today for $10,000 but realize it is a lemon and dispose of it for $9,000, you have a $1,000 capital loss.

Taxation of capital gains—the basics

What you paid for an asset is often, in accounting lingo, referred to as its basis. That may sound complicated, but we can simplify it. Basis is simply what you paid for an asset, plus any other costs you incurred to acquire it, including sales taxes, commissions, shipping and handling costs, and installation charges. It also includes the cost of improvements. So if you buy a house for $100,000 and spend $50,000 improving it, your basis is $150,000. (Depreciation of an asset, on the other hand, can reduce your basis. But we do not need to go into detail about that here.)

So how are capital gains taxed? First, you have to decide if the capital gain is long term or short term. If you hold the asset for more than one year before you dispose of it, your capital gain or loss is long term. If you hold the asset for one year or less, your capital gain or loss is short term. To determine how long you held the asset, simply begin counting from the day after you acquired the asset up to and including the day you disposed of the asset.

The reason the length of time you held an asset is important is that long-term and short-term capital gains are taxed at different rates. Short-term capital gains are taxed at the same rate as ordinary income. Long-term capital gains are taxed at a much lower rate. The table below illustrates.

Taxation of Long-Term Capital Gains (2022)

Filing Status	0% Rate	15% Rate	20% Rate
Single	Up to $41,675	$41,676 – $459,750	Over $459,750
Married filing jointly	Up to $83,350	$83,351 – $517,200	Over $517,200

Why are capital gains taxed lower than ordinary income taxes, you might ask? It is because the government wants citizens to be long-term investors. Investment helps drive the economy forward and benefits everyone, the theory goes.

Finally, note that while there is a difference between dividends and capital gains, the tax treatment is currently similar. In the past, common stock dividends were taxed at ordinary income tax rates. When the Jobs and Growth Tax Relief Reconciliation Act of 2003 was passed, however, dividends began receiving the same tax treatment as long-term capital gains. That led many companies to implement or raise dividends to make their stocks more appealing.

Why do I pay capital gains tax when I didn't sell my fund?

It is a common question from mutual fund investors. You held your mutual fund throughout the year, but your fund company still sends you a capital-gains tax report come January. Why? Mutual funds consist of many different stocks or bonds. During the year, the fund manager buys and sells securities. Some of these transactions result in gains and others in losses. At the end of the year, if there is a net capital gain on what the portfolio manager sold, that gain is passed on to shareholders.

Offsetting capital gains with losses

Any investment professional can (and should) tell you that investments do not always rise in value. Sometimes they fall. As noted earlier, in this case, you have a capital loss. And capital losses can be deducted from capital gains in the case of investments.

As an example, if you have $10,000 in long-term gains from the sale of one investment but $3,000 in long-term losses from the sale of another, you only have to pay taxes only on $7,000 worth of long-term capital gains.

You can offset up to $3,000 of capital gains per year with capital losses. If you have more than $3,000 in capital losses in any given year, you can carry them forward indefinitely until you have used them all.

Now there are some nuances to capital-gains taxes as is usually the case with investments. For example, capital gains on artwork and collectibles are taxed as ordinary income up to a maximum rate of 28 percent. You may also exclude up to 50 percent of capital gains on stock held for more than five years in a domestic *C* corporation with gross assets under $50 million on the date of the stock's issuance. But let's not get into the nitty-gritty; that is an accountant's forte.

401(k) plans and capital gains

One caveat regarding capital gains and losses pertains to 401(k) plans. If you realize a capital gain inside a 401(k), it is not taxed as a capital gain. It is taxed at the usually higher ordinary income tax rate when you withdraw it. Additionally, if you realize a capital loss in a 401(k), you cannot offset it against a capital loss as you would be able to outside a 401(k).

Let's make that simple with an example. Say Jane invests $10,000 into a growth fund outside a 401(k) plan, and Bob invests $10,000 into the same growth fund inside his 401(k) plan.

What happens if the value of the fund rises to $13,000, and Jane and Bob sell at the exact same time? Jane pays a capital gains tax of 0 percent to 20 percent on the $3,000 profit, depending on her income-tax bracket. Bob doesn't pay any capital gains now but pays income tax on the earnings (10 percent to 37 percent) later when he withdraws the money from his 401(k) plan.

Now, what happens if the value of the fund falls to $7,000, and Jane and Bob sell at the exact same time? Jane gets a tax deduction she can use against her income. Bob gets nothing but less money in retirement when he starts to make withdrawals from his 401(k) plan. Who got the better deal? I say Jane because in essence, by investing via a 401(k) plan, you are eliminating the lower capital-gains tax and replacing it with the much higher income tax.

Why you have been swindled

Let's say you make an investment in your 401(k) plan and believe—because you have been told so—that any gain you realize will not be exposed to capital-gains tax because it occurred inside your 401(k) plan. You have been misled. It is true that you will not have to pay capital-gains taxes on profitable investments made inside a 401(k) plan. But material information has been omitted. What would have been a capital gain had the investment occurred outside a 401(k) plan is now earned income and taxable at the much higher federal tax rate (and state tax rate)! Capital gains, meanwhile, are not taxed at the state level in any single state.

Your home—exempt from capital gains?

Most Americans' largest single asset is their home. Depending on how long you own a home and how the real estate market performed during that time, you might realize a significant capital gain on its sale. The good news: You can exclude up to $250,000 of the capital gain on your home sale if you are single, $500,000 if you are married filing jointly—provided certain conditions are met. First, you must have owned the home for at least two years in the five-year period before the sale. Second, the home must have been your primary residence for at least two years in that same five-year period. Finally, you cannot have excluded the capital gain from another home sale in the two-year period before the sale.

Business income versus capital gains

If you operate a business, you may be tempted to report your business income as a capital gain. But it is not. Say you buy old furniture, spiff it up, and sell it on Etsy. While the money you pay for the old furniture is a business expense, the money you receive in sales in revenue and the difference between the two is considered income. Your profit is therefore subject to income tax, not capital gains tax.

Managing taxes with tax-managed funds

Everyone wants to get ahead of Uncle Sam, and if you're an investor, one way to do so (legally) is to invest in tax-managed mutual funds.

Taxation basics

The reason pertains to how mutual funds are taxed.

When you think of paying taxes in your mutual fund investments, you're probably thinking of capital-gains taxes levied on your own sale of shares of the fund.

When you sell your mutual fund shares for more than you paid for them, you realize either a short-term or a long-term capital gain. But there's another kind of tax when it comes to mutual funds: embedded gains that are distributed to shareholders each year. Inside the mutual fund, the portfolio manager is constantly buying and selling securities. When a portfolio manager buys and sells securities at a gain, the mutual fund incurs a tax bill, and those taxes are passed on the shareholders (you) at the end of the year.

That's true even if you have all of your capital gains and dividends reinvested.

That's true even if you've only owned the fund for a short period of time.

Say it isn't so!

It's so. Let's say you invested last week and have all gains and dividends reinvested. Well, the mutual fund may have purchased a stock a long time ago, and now it sells that stock. You participate in your proportional share of the capital gain, so you also owe taxes on that gain.

That's right—even if you didn't sell and fund shares, you will still receive a 1099 form that shows the amount of your gain, and you will have to report the gain on your tax return and pay the applicable taxes.

Sometimes, your mutual fund can be down for the year, and you'll still owe taxes because of the trading activity in the portfolio—a bit of a double punch in the gut.

Enter tax-managed funds

At some point in history, someone figured out that investors don't like that and invested in the tax-managed or tax-efficient mutual fund. These funds are designed to minimize the tax liability that shareholders face.

With a tax-managed mutual fund, the portfolio manager seeks to minimize capital gains distributions in a number of ways. He or she may minimize the fund's turnover, especially if the fund invests in stocks. Stocks held for more than one year are taxed at a lower long-term capital-gains rate. Typically, when the fund manager sells an investment at a profit (gain), they try to match it up with a corresponding loss. This technique will neutralize the gain thus eliminating the taxes due.

If you compare tax-managed mutual funds to the typical actively managed mutual fund, they are, indeed, dramatically more tax efficient.

Where to find tax-managed funds

Many mutual funds companies offer funds that are designated as tax-managed.

Vanguard Tax-Managed Capital Appreciation Fund has $16.6 billion in assets under management as of June 30, 2021. The portfolio's benchmark is the domestic Russell 1000 Index, though portfolio managers can make adjustments for dividend levels and other tax factors, such as taking advantage of losses. The turnover is 6.0 percent and the expense ratio is 0.09 percent as of June 30, 2021. And since the fund was launched in 2001, there has never been a capital-gains distribution. (Other tax-managed Vanguard options include Vanguard Tax-Managed Small Cap Fund and Vanguard Tax-Managed Balanced Fund.)

Vanguard Tax-Managed Balanced Fund is another Vanguard option if you're looking for a mix of stocks and bonds. It provides exposure to the mid- and large-cap segments of the US stock market with about 50 percent of its assets, investing the balance in federally tax-exempt municipal bonds. The fund has $7.9 billion in assets under management as of June 30, 2021, and its expense ratio is just 0.09 percent.

T. Rowe Price Tax-Efficient Equity Fund has $877 million in assets under management as of June 30, 2021. More growth-oriented than the Vanguard fund, the portfolio's benchmark is the Russell 3000 Growth Index, and the fund expects to have significant investments in technology companies. The turnover is 13.50, and the expense ratio is 0.78 percent.

Fidelity Tax-Free Bond Fund is a good option if you're in the market for a bond fund. It holds municipal bonds, which are exempt from federal income tax. While municipal bonds generally have lower yields than corporate bonds, the tax-free status can produce a tax-effective yield that can beat other bonds. Generally, investors who are in higher tax brackets benefit the most from holding municipal bond funds. The fund has $4.6 billion in assets under management as of June 30, 2021, and its expense ratio is 0.25 percent.

Russell Tax-Managed U.S. Large Cap Fund is another big one with $5.6 billion in assets under management as of June 30, 2021. A core fund (a blend of growth and value), it invests in other funds whose managers have inherently tax-sensitive investment approaches. If you like that idea, Russell has several other offerings that use the same multi-manager approach, including Russell Tax-Managed US Mid and Small Cap Fund and Russell Tax-Managed International Equity Fund.

Blackrock iShares ETFs are an option if you prefer to go the route of index funds or ETFs, discusses in "cons" above. Blackrock has more than 393 ETFs traded in the United States and more than $2.3 trillion in ETF assets under management as of June 30, 2021, so there's sure to be an iShares ETF for you.

To determine how much you will save in a tax-managed fund versus other funds, you can review the mutual fund's statistics regarding a fund's historic tax costs.

Stepping up in basis

One more thing worth exploring when discussing the capital-gains tax is gifts. The basis for an asset you received as a gift is equivalent to the donor's basis. So if your parents buy a cottage for $80,000 then give it to you ten years later when it is valued at $120,000, the basis is still $80,000.

But what about inheritances? Aha! That is different. The basis of an inherited asset is "stepped up" to the value of the asset on the date of the donor's death. So if your parents buy a cottage for $80,000 then die when it is valued at $120,000, at which point you inherit it, your basis is $120,000.

Why is there a discrepancy between gifts and inheritances? Uncle Sam is being nice. The provision of the tax code that allows inheritances to be treated differently essentially exempts from taxes any gains on assets held until someone's death.

The step-up in basis is a commonly overlooked tax benefit that can help minimize taxes. While gifting is often the preferred means of transferring wealth, you may want to be wary of gifting significantly appreciated assets during your lifetime as it could result in capital-gains taxes. These taxes could be avoided by allowing the assets to be transferred as an inheritance.

Consider how the step-up in basis might apply to investments. Say you purchase a share of stock for $1, and the value grows to $100 at which time you sell it. You would be responsible for paying capital gains tax on the $99 gain you received from this sale. Now, let's say instead of selling the stock, you die and leave it to your child when it is worth $100. Your child gets a new cost basis of $100. If he or she then sells the stock for $100, there is no capital gain. Your child has received the stock tax free. The step-up in basis erased the capital gains and the tax liability that would have accompanied it.

In summary, the step-up in basis is a simple concept. If you received a capital asset from another person because of his or her death, the cost basis (in essence, what the deceased paid for it) is the value of the asset at the time of the death. I believe it is the single biggest tax break in the entire tax code.

But it is never simple when it comes to taxes, is it? In some cases, a half step-up can apply. Let's say two spouses purchased stock for $50,000 and held it as joint tenants with rights of survivorship. One spouse passes away, at which time the stock is worth $100,000. In this case, a partial increase in basis may apply. The new basis for the surviving spouse would be equal to the fair market value on the date of death ($100,000) plus the original basis ($50,000) divided by two—so $75,000. In other words, half of the assets receive a stepped-up basis. But it may be best to leave that one to an accountant.

No step-up for 401(k)s

I believe the step-up in basis is the single biggest tax break in the entire tax code—but it doesn't apply to 401(k) plans, which is another reason to avoid them. If you are like most Americans, most of your retirement assets are held in 401(k) plans or Individual Retirement Account (IRAs). The assets held in a tax-deferred retirement plan such as these do not receive a step-up in cost basis. That is because all distributions from tax-deferred retirement plans—to you or to a beneficiary—are taxed as ordinary income.

Chapter 11

Save, Withdraw, and Pass It On—*Tax Free*

People feel like the system is rigged against them, and here is the painful part: they're right.

—Elizabeth Warren

I already told you how I feel about 401(k) plans in chapter 10, but in this chapter, I will discuss them in light of taxes, distributions, and inheritances—and show you how to use three important tax laws to create a *tax-free* retirement and estate.

Keep in mind, I am writing this for the 99 percent of us, not for the top 1 percent. They "earned" out of this option many billions of dollars ago. That's why they have a team of lawyers and CPAs. You and I don't have that "problem." My techniques are designed for the rest of us who just want to improve our financial lives and make sure we are applying all the current tax codes properly.

Rules for the 99 percent

The gig RetireSmart plan comes down to following three simple IRS rules:

Rule #1: standard deduction 2022 ($12,950 annual tax-free max). We all get $12,950 of tax-free income a year. The problem is we all use it to reduce our taxes today by a small amount. How much? For most of us, it's approximately $100 per month. I say, go out to dinner less once a month and apply that deduction to your retirement years. In fact, the proof that my logic is sound is the rise of Roth IRAs. A Roth IRA is funded by after-tax dollars. The Smart 401(k) is like a Roth 401(k) on steroids.

Rule #2: distribution, capital gains ($41,675 annual tax-free max). By applying your standard deduction each year to your retirement savings and investing it in a tax-managed account, you will now be able to withdraw money using the capital gain tax rates. This means you can withdraw (in this example) $54,625 from your account. For the first $12,950, you can apply your standard deduction, and the remaining $41,675 is taxed at the capital gain rate. Your total federal taxes due: $0 (zero).

Rule #3: at death, step-up in basis ($11.4 million life tax-free max). The step-up rule is the golden goose for the rich. It simply means that you can pass after-tax appreciated assets to your heir's tax free. The 2022 limit on this exemption is $12.06 million per person. No problem!

So to review, note the following:

1. Use your standard deduction to "fund" your after-tax retirement account today.
2. Invest it in special low-cost tax-managed mutual funds. Pull money out tax free (limit applies) as needed.
3. Pass on to heirs using the step-up in basis.

For 99 percent of us, I just showed you how to save *tax free*, withdraw *tax free*, and pass it on *tax free*.

The "appeal" of 401(k) plans

Today, the old-school retirement plans known as defined-benefit plans or pensions are rare. The 401(k) plans—which allow employees to contribute funds to a qualified retirement plan via a pretax reduction in salary—have been a staple of retirement saving since they were created by the Revenue Act of 1978 and went into effect on January 1, 1980. There are other similar tax-deductible plans for nonprofit organizations, but all are designed to create an incentive for retirement saving by deferring wage earners' income taxes until a future date.

It's easy to understand why 401(k) plans are so attractive. They allow employees to save up to $20,500 under the age of fifty and $27,000 over the age of fifty a year, pretax, and direct the manner in which it's invested (with an additional $6,500 catch-up contribution allowed for those age fifty and older). Earnings derived from the investments in the plan are not taxed; they're reinvested and compound over time.

In 2006, a new type of 401(k) plan became available—the Roth. Roth 401(k) plans allow wage earners to contribute after-tax funds to a retirement plan. Contributions have already been taxed, so withdrawals of those contributions in retirement are tax free (and there's the possibility that investment earnings could qualify for a nontaxable distribution as well). That offers another level of flexibility for individuals who want more spendable income in retirement.

With both traditional and Roth 401(k) plans, employees can invest in stocks, bonds, or a combination of stocks and bonds, depending on the level of risk the employee can tolerate.

Adding to the appeal of 401(k) plans, many employers match part of an employee's contribution. According to Aon's 2015 Trends and Experience in DC Plans Survey, 42 percent of companies match employees' 401(k) contributions dollar-for-dollar, up from 31 percent in 2013.

Another benefit of 401(k) plans is that they offer some flexibility if you're in a financial pinch. You have two options.

First, you can take a loan from your 401(k) plan, if permitted by the plan (and 87 percent of 401(k) plans offer loan options, according to the Employee Benefit Research Institute, or EBRI). Such loans typically allow you to borrow up to 50 percent of your account balance up to a maximum of $50,000. You must repay the loan within five years unless you're using the money for a down payment on a home, in which case the repayment period is longer. And typically, you repay the loan through automatic deductions from your paycheck. It's a great option if you need a loan because instead of paying interest to a bank, you're paying it to yourself.

Second, IRS rules allow you to take what's called a hardship withdrawal from your 401(k) plan (though your employer has to allow it as well).

Acceptable reasons for a hardship withdrawal, according to the IRS, are (1) unreimbursed medical expenses for you, your spouse, or dependents; (2) purchase of your principal residence; (3) payment of college tuition and related educational costs for you, your spouse, dependents, or children who are no longer dependents; (4) payments necessary to prevent the eviction of you from your home or foreclosure on the mortgage of your principal residence; (5) funeral expenses; and (6) certain expenses for the repair of damage to your principal residence.

Such hardship withdrawals are subject to income tax and, if you are not at least fifty-nine and a half years of age, a 10 percent withdrawal penalty.

Hardship withdrawals are penalty free if you meet any one of a number of specific requirements—for example, you become totally disabled, you're in debt for medical expenses that exceed 7.5 percent of your adjusted gross income, or you're required by court order to pay funds to a spouse, child, or dependent. Other acceptable reasons for a penalty-free hardship withdrawal include (a) permanent layoff, termination, quitting, or early retirement in the same year you turn fifty-five; or (b) permanent layoff, termination, quitting, or retirement accompanied by payments for the rest of your (or your designated beneficiaries') life or life expectancy that continues for at least five years or until you reach age fifty-nine and a half, whichever is longer.

With such features, 401(k) plans are extremely popular. Many financial pundits—financial advisors, corporate human resources managers, and financial institutions—tout their advantages as a great way to save for retirement.

And individual investors listen. According to the most recent statistics from the US Department of Labor (as of December 2018), there are 656,241 defined contribution retirement plans in the United States, 560,241 of which are 401(k) plans. Nearly 90 percent of full-time workers have access to employer-sponsored retirement plans and most workers participate in a plan. One survey from the Plan Sponsor Council of America found that the average percentage of eligible employees with a balance in a defined-contribution plan is 88.7 percent.

As of the first quarter of 2021, US retirement assets in defined contribution plans were $9.9 trillion, of which $6.9 trillion was held in 401(k) plans, according to the Investment Company Institute (out of $35.4 trillion in total retirement assets).

But then there are the management fees.

The truth about your 401 (dismay)!

Hey, brace yourself because the advice I'm about to give you may seem like financial heresy: stop contributing to your 401(k) plan immediately!

You read that right, and the reason is that investing in your 401(k) plan is a mistake that could cost you and your loved ones hundreds of thousands of dollars in taxes.

I've studied this topic extensively. So far, however, my theory hasn't gained any traction. I've spoken to clients, certified public accountants (CPAs), and even an IRS agent about it. One CPA looked me square in the eye and said, "You're nuts!"

Am I nuts or just not brainwashed?

Throughout our working lives, we've all been taught to save money for retirement via a 401(k) plan. The pitch goes something like this: You get a tax deduction today, and the money grows tax deferred. Then when you withdraw the money in retirement, you'll likely be in a lower tax bracket. In the end, then, you reduce how much you pay in taxes.

What do I think about that argument? It's wrong! The problem with the traditional logic is that it doesn't tell you how things will work out in the end. It's like Evel Knievel telling you how easy it is to jump a motorcycle over fifty buses. The jumping is easy; it's the landing that can be very painful.

Similarly, when it comes to 401(k) plans, people generally talk about only the accumulation phase (the jump); no one is willing to talk about the distribution phase (the landing). I, however, am going to present you with both the jump and the landing—proving in the process that a 401(k) plan will generate more tax revenue for the IRS than an investment in an after-tax account. Hold on tight because you're in for quite a ride. But I promise we will stick to the landing.

Brief disclosure: there are more than one hundred million tax filers in the United States. Even though we all use the same tax code, just like snowflakes, there are no two tax returns that are identical. I guarantee you that there are many folks whose individual situations would make my approach fruitless. However, the vast majority of Americans would, no doubt, benefit from what I am about to present to you. Also, the following does not include the impact a company match would have on the outcome.

So sit back in your most comfortable chair with your favorite beverage and open your mind because you're about to see behind the curtain how the wealthy get that way—and just as importantly, stay that way.

Meet Mr. Uninformed and Mrs. Smart

To make my point, I'll run two different scenarios—one for Mr. Uninformed and one for Mrs. Smart. Both invested $1,000 per month from August 1979 until August 2009. Both invested in Vanguard 500 Index Fund (VFINX), a mutual fund that tracks the S&P 500 Index so investment performance was identical. Both ended up with $1,781,538 in their accounts.

It should be noted that the 401(k) contribution limit in 1979 was below $12,000 annually. I chose the 1979–2009 time period because most retirees' savings are the result of thirty years of building their nest egg.

However, Mr. Uninformed invested his money in a traditional 401(k) plan, and Mrs. Smart invested her money in an after-tax account, which is an account funded with after-tax dollars.

Here's where the fun begins.

Phase 1: accumulation (standard deduction). Under new tax laws, the IRS allows all individual filers to deduct the first $12,950 of their earned income each year. Joint filers can deduct $25,900. So that means when Mr. Uninformed contributed the $1,000 a month ($12,000 annually) to his 401(k), this was money that wasn't going to be taxed anyway. But now it is in a tax-deferred account.

Mrs. Smart also used $12,000 to fund her after-tax account.

Let's summarize: Mr. Uniformed put $12,000 into his 401(k) and paid $0 in taxes on the money. Now the $12,000 is in a tax-deferred account, so all growth on the money will be taxed as income when he withdraws it.

Mrs. Smart put $12,000 into her after-tax account and paid no taxes on the money. Now the $12,000 is in an after-tax account, so all growth on the money will be taxed as capital gains when she withdraws it.

Since both invested their contributions in the exact same investment on the same day, they ended up with exactly the amount of money. See below.

Mr. Uniformed Meets Mrs. Smart

	Mr. Uninformed	Mrs. Smart
401(k) plan	$1,781,538	$0
Tax-managed after- tax account	$0	$1,781,358
Net value at retirement	$1,781,538	$1,781,538

So there is no winner, right? So far, it certainly looks that way because if by the time you retire, you have accumulated the same amount of money in a 401(k) plan as you would in an after-tax account, the 401(k) plan must be the best option, most people would say.

Phase 2: distribution (capital gain). But wait a moment. Let's look at what happens as Mr. Uninformed and Mrs. Smart progress into retirement. Both investors start a systematic withdrawal program, taking $36,000 a year from their nest eggs. And here's where we begin to see a difference.

Mr. Uninformed withdraws $36,000 and receives a 1099-R at the end of the year. A 1099-R is a tax form used to report distributions from annuities, profit-sharing plans, retirement plans, IRAs, insurance contracts, and pension plans. It is required by the IRS from any individual who has a distribution of more than $10.

The 1099-R cues the IRS that Mr. Uninformed withdrew $36,000 from his 401(k), and he needs to add that to his current tax return. As with his contribution, the first $12,950 is deductible thus tax free. That leaves Mr. Uninformed to pay ordinary income tax on the remaining $23,050. The table below shows his taxes due. Please note that all the income above these thresholds will be subject to ordinary income tax. However, the first $12,950 withdrawn are income and capital gain free.

Mr. Uninformed's Tax Bill

	401(k) Plan
Withdrawal	$36,000
Standard deduction	$12,950
Taxable income	$23,050
Tax bracket	12%
Federal income tax due	$2,560.50

Meanwhile, Mrs. Smart withdraws the same $36,000 from her after-tax account. The same $12,950 deduction applies. However, her balance of $23,050 is taxed as capital gains, not as ordinary income. The table below shows her taxes due.

Mrs. Smart's Tax Bill

	Tax-Managed Account
Withdrawal	$36,000
Standard deduction	$12,950
Taxable capital gain (at 0%)	$23,050
Taxable income	$0
Capital gains tax due	$0

Yes, you read that correctly. Mrs. Smart owes $0 in income tax and $0 in capital gains tax.

I know, most of you are saying that can't be correct. There is no way this is possible.

Well, America, it is correct, and it is possible! How?

Not all capital gains are treated equally. The tax rate can vary dramatically between short-term and long-term gains.

Short-term capital gains—those on assets you have held for one year or less—do not benefit from any special tax rate. They are taxed at the same rate as your ordinary income.

Long-term capital gains—those on assets you have held for longer than a year—are reduced. The taxes are 0 percent, 15 percent, or 20 percent for most taxpayers, depending on their tax bracket. Mrs. Smart's tax bracket was low enough that she had a 0 percent tax rate on capital gains. Mr. Uninformed, on the other hand, didn't receive this benefit.

Whether you generate a short-term or long-term gain in a tax-advantaged account, you don't have to pay any tax until you take the money out of the account—but everything you withdraw, even profits from long-term capital gains, are taxable as ordinary income. Essentially, you obtain the benefit of tax deferral but lose the benefit of the long-term capital gains tax rate.

Phase 3: death (step-up in basis). Now, let's say ten years go by, and Mr. Uninformed and Mrs. Smart see their money grow by the same amount. Both make annual withdrawals of $36,000, and Mr. Uninformed pays roughly $26,895 ($2,689.50 times ten) on those withdrawals while Mrs. Smart pays $0.

Then tragedy strikes, and both Mr. Uninformed and Mrs. Smart pass away. Upon their death, each has $1,781,538 left, and those funds are distributed to their beneficiaries, who, we will assume, are their children, and pay no estate taxes.

The distribution from Mr. Uninformed's account is considered income to his children, and that distribution is a taxable event. As a result, Mr. Uninformed's children are hit with a tax bill of $427,569 (assuming a tax bracket of 24 percent at the federal level and 0 percent at the state level). In the end, Mr. Uninformed children's net inheritance is only $1,327,075. Remember, this assumes a 0 zero percent state income tax which only a handful of have.

Now, let's look at what happens to Mrs. Smart's beneficiaries, whom we will assume are her children. She did not receive a 1099-R and gets to keep all the $1,781,538 in her account. Why? Because upon Mrs. Smart's death, her children get what is called a step-up in cost basis to the value of the account at the date of death—a provision that does not apply to retirement accounts such as Mr. Uninformed. That may sound complicated, but it simply refers to the adjustment of the cost of an appreciated asset, upon inheritance, for tax purposes. With a step-up in cost basis, the value of the asset is the market value of the asset at the time of inheritance, not the market value at which the asset was purchased—and the former is usually higher. As a result, Mrs. Smart's tax bill at death is $0, and her children net $1,781,538.

The Big Picture

	Mr. Uninformed	Mrs. Smart
Accumulation at death	$1,781,538	$1,781,538
Taxes paid at death	$427,569	$0
Net value at death	$1,327,075	$1,781,538
Difference		$454,463

So Mrs. Smart's beneficiary netted $454,463 more than Mr. Uninformed's beneficiary. Pretty good, right? Well, it gets even better for Mrs. Smart if you look at how much total she paid in taxes over the years relative to Mr. Uninformed.

The Bigger Picture

	Mr. Uninformed	Mrs. Smart
Taxes paid during accumulation phase	$0	$0
Taxes paid during distribution phase	$26,895	$0
Taxes paid at death	$427,569	$0
Total taxes paid	$456,449	$0

You must be asking yourself, "How can this be? This isn't what I was told all these years." But there's a reason Mrs. Smart came out ahead. It's not because she possessed an incredible ability to manage the stock market. Remember, Mrs. Smart and Mr. Uninformed invested in exactly the same investments on exactly the same days. Mrs. Smart came out ahead because she understood the tax laws and how to use them to her advantage.

That reminds me of the time Warren Buffett, considered by most to be the greatest stock picker the world has ever known, said his secretary is in a higher tax bracket than he is. Now you know why he said that.

Mrs. Smart's capital losses

Mrs. Smart has another advantage over Mr. Uninformed.

If your investments end up losing money rather than generating capital gains, you can use those losses to reduce your taxes.

You simply match up your gains and losses in any given year to determine your net capital gain or loss. If you end up with a net loss, you can use up to $3,000 per year to reduce your taxable income. If you have a net loss of more than $3,000, you can carry it forward to future tax years, to either offset capital gains or ordinary income.

But that's only possible in an after-tax account. Because you don't generate capital gains or losses in a retirement account, you can't use capital losses to offset capital gains or income.

A little more sizzle

If that's not enough to convince you that investing in a 401(k) plan isn't a good idea, let's add some more sizzle to this steak. During both the accumulation and distribution phases—meaning before and after retirement—Mrs. Smart can withdraw money at any time from her account without paying a penny in income taxes, penalties, or excise taxes. So if Mrs. Smart needs to make a big purchase or encounters some kind of financial hardship, such as significant medical bills, she can easily get to her money. Whether she needs $500 or $50,000, she can touch it at any time for any reason. Mr. Uninformed, however, has to jump through government-created hoops—which include claiming hardship, making in-service withdrawals, and taking loans—to touch the smallest amount of his money.

What about loans?

But what about loans, you may ask. Mr. Uninformed could easily, if necessary, take a loan from his 401(k) plan to access his money. Traditional wisdom holds that taking a loan from your own 401(k) plan is a good idea because in doing so, you are actually paying yourself back with interest. And the interest rate is typically low, usually around the prime rate plus 1 percent.

But there are some difficulties with 401(k) plan loans. You typically have to borrow at least $1,000, and you usually can't borrow more than 50 percent of your account balance (to a maximum of $50,000). You can borrow only the vested amount, meaning your unvested company contributions are off-limits. The maximum loan term is five years. You generally cannot have more than one loan at a time, meaning you must borrow what you need the first time.

That's a lot of obstacles! And even if you can overcome all of those obstacles, there will likely be a loan origination fee and an annual administration fee. Then if you are unable to pay back your loan, the IRS will view the unpaid balance as an early withdrawal and hit you with a 10 percent penalty.

What catch-up contributions?

You may also wonder about catch-up contributions. Do they make investing in 401(k) plans more appealing?

Just to ensure we're on the same page, a 401(k) plan may permit participants who are age fifty or over at the end of a calendar year to make an elective contribution beyond the general limits that apply to 401(k) plans. These contributions are commonly referred to as catch-up contributions.

You may or may not be able to make a catch-up contribution because an employer is not required to provide for catch-up contributions in any of its plans.

However, if your plan does allow for catch-up contributions, here are the general rules: If you participate in a traditional or so-called safe harbor 401(k) plan and you are age fifty or older, the catch-up contribution is $7,000 as of 2022. If you participate in a Savings Incentive Match Plan for Employees of Small Employers (SIMPLE) 401(k) plan and you are age fifty or older, the catch-up contribution is $3,000 as of 2022.

Assuming you can make such contributions, is investing in a 401(k) plan still a bad idea? Yes, and for the same reasons I've already stated. Being able to contribute more money doesn't make a difference. A tax-managed account has no limits on contributions or on catch-up contributions. If you win the lottery, you can put as much as 100 percent of the windfall in a tax-managed account and multiply the benefits.

Another reason to watch out—automatic enrollments

When left to their own devices, many employees don't contribute to their 401(k) plans, or they contribute just enough to qualify for matching funds their employers may offer, usually 6 percent or less.

That may not be enough to fund a solid retirement since many financial planners say employees should aim to save at least 10 percent or more of their pretax earnings over their working lives to ensure an adequate retirement nest egg.

Indeed, a sizable percentage of US workers say they have virtually no money in retirement savings. According to the EBRI's 2016

Retirement Confidence Survey, 54 percent of US workers report that the total value of their household's savings and investments, excluding the value of their primary home and any defined-benefit plans, is less than $25,000. And about half of households age fifty-five and older have no retirement savings, according to a June 2015 report from the Government Accountability Office (GAO).

Why? People just aren't contributing to their 401(k) plans. While 53 percent of US workers are offered a plan by their current employer, just 45 percent say they contribute money, according to the EBRI's 2016 Retirement Confidence Survey. And according to the same EBRI survey, just 21 percent of US workers are "very confident" they'll have enough money saved for a comfortable retirement.

As a result, many employers automatically enroll employees in their 401(k) plans—i.e., they opt them in—thanks to the Pension Protection Act (PPA) of 2006, which removed many of the legal barriers to automatically enroll eligible employees in such plans. According to Aon's 2015 Trends and Experience in DC Plans Survey, 52 percent of employers automatically enroll workers at a savings rate of 4 percent or more, up from 39 percent of employers in 2013.

A similar feature is an automatic escalation in which a 401(k) plan, usually at the start of each year, automatically raises the percentage of pay that plan participants contribute by 1 percent or more until they achieve a set deferral rate, such as 10 percent.

That doesn't mean employees give up their rights to enroll or not enroll, or how much to contribute; it just means that if they don't want to participate or participate less, they have to opt out.

The data on opt-ins and opt-outs varies. According to a 2015 survey report by the Defined Contribution Institutional Investment Association (DCIIA), 62 percent of employers with large plans (more than $200 million in assets) automatically enroll new employees into their plan while 48 percent of smaller employers do. But retirement services firm Ascensus says only 18 percent of the forty-thousand-plus retirement plans serviced by it automatically enroll their employees.

There's some evidence that automatic enrollment works. According to Ascensus, only around 1 percent of workers that are automatically enrolled into a retirement plan choose to opt out.

That's one reason President Obama, when in office, proposed new rules around automatic enrollments. He wanted employers with more than ten workers to automatically enroll employees in an individual retirement account (IRA) if they didn't provide another type of retirement benefit. And he wanted to give companies with one hundred or fewer employees who did so a tax credit of up to $3,000. He didn't succeed. The legislative branch didn't take the bait.

But given the problems with 401(k) plans I've described above, do you really want to be enrolled without your consent?

One exception

Now you may have one more question. What if your company matches 401(k) plan contributions? Does that still mean investing in a 401(k) plan is a bad idea? First, fewer and fewer companies are matching 401(k) plan contributions these days. But if you're one of the lucky few employees who receive a match, the answer is that investing in a 401(k) plan isn't quite such a bad idea. But you should invest only up to the level of the company match. In other words, if your company matches up to 4 percent, contribute 4 percent and not a penny more.

Snapshot: Traditional 401(k) versus Roth 401(k) versus 1099(m) Plan

	Traditional 401(k)	Roth 401(k)	1099(m)
Eligibility Age	21	21	At birth
Contribution Limits	$20,500* * In 2022.	$20,500* * In 2022.	Unlimited
Catch-Up Contributions (Age 50+)	$7,000* * In 2019.	$7,000* * In 2019.	Unlimited
Employer Match	Allowed, if offered by the employer	Allowed, if offered by the employer	Unavailable

The Ins and Outs of Taxes

Contribution Taxation	Pre-tax	After-tax	After-tax
Investment options	Limited to plan menu; usually 10 to 20 choices	Limited to plan menu; usually 10 to 20 choices	Unlimited
Investment advice	Limited	Limited	Yes
Withdrawal taxation	All withdrawals taxed as income	Earnings taxed as income before five years and under age 59 1/2	Taxed as short-term capital gain less than one year
Tax rate	As income: rates 10% to 37%	As income: rates 10% to 35%	As capital gain: rates 0% to 20%
Excise tax	10% under age 59 1/2	10% on growth under age 59 1/2	0%
Access	Not until age 59 1/2	Not until age 59 1/2 and have held account for more than five years	Anytime
Penalty-free distributions before age 59 1/2	No	No	Yes
Required minimum distributions	Begin age 72 1/2 or when the account holder retires, whichever comes later	Begin age 72 1/2 or when the account holder retires, whichever comes later	None
Taxes at death	100% taxed at income	Tax-free provided all IRS requirements are met	Tax-free

Five reasons to invest in after-tax accounts

In summary, here's why you should invest in a tax-advantaged after-tax account instead of a 401(k) plan.

You're taxed at the capital gains level. When the government established 401(k) plans in 1980, it ran projections showing that if you get a tax deduction at the time of investment, if the assets grow tax-deferred, and if you withdraw the money at a lower tax rate, you end up with more money. The government was right in those projections. However—and this is a huge however—the government changed the rules along the way. It lowered the capital gains tax rate. When 401(k) plans were established, income and capital gains were taxed at the same rate. Today and for the foreseeable future, federal income is taxed at a maximum of 37 percent, and capital gains are taxed at a maximum of 20 percent. So at the time of distribution and death, the money in your 401(k) plan will always be taxed at the higher income rate and not at the lower capital gains rate.

It allows for a step-up in cost basis. To recap, a step-up in cost basis is a tax code provision that allows the cost of an appreciated asset, upon inheritance, to be adjusted for tax purposes. With a step-up in cost basis, the value of the asset is the market value of the asset at the time of inheritance, not the market value at which the asset was purchased—and the former is usually higher. The step-up in cost basis is the single biggest tax break the IRS gives us, and it does not apply to retirement accounts.

You get to choose exactly what you want to sell. You probably know what cost basis is: essentially, the original value of an investment (usually the purchase price). The difference between the cost basis of an investment and its current market value is your capital gain. Often, when selling an investment, investors will choose which "lot" to sell based on a cost basis. For example, let's say you have one hundred shares of stock. You purchased fifty shares at $50 a share, and fifty shares at $100 a share. Now, you want to sell fifty shares at the market price of $125 per share. Chances are you'd choose to sell the lot of shares you purchased at $100 because then your capital gain would be only $25 per share. But that matters only in an after-tax account. With a 401(k) plan, all before-tax contributions have a cost basis of zero. As a result, it doesn't matter which ones you withdraw, and every dollar withdrawn is taxed as income. You lose an important means of managing your investments for tax efficiency.

You have total access to your money. Tax-managed accounts have none of the withdrawal restrictions 401(k) plans do. You can access any amount of money you want, at any time.

In conclusion, your long-term investments must navigate not only the markets but also the tax code—and as long as the tax code is structured so that income is taxed at a higher rate than capital gains and there's a step-up in cost basis for after-tax accounts, your 401(k) plan will likely be the most taxed of all your assets. Now that you know better, don't invest in a 401(k) plan. In avoiding this tax trap, you'll be joining every member of Congress. They don't have 401(k) plans either. Maybe that should tell you something.

You aren't subject to required minimum distributions (RMDs). An RMD is, in many ways, the WMD (weapon of mass destruction) of retirement planning. It is a minimum amount of money you must withdraw annually from your retirement account, typically starting in the year that you reach seventy and a half years of age. RMDs apply to all employer-sponsored retirement plans, including profit-sharing plans, 401(k) plans, 403(b) plans, and 457(b) plans, as well as to traditional IRAs and IRA-based plans such as SEPs and SIMPLE IRAs. If you don't want to withdraw your money so it can keep growing, this could be a problem. That's another reason after-tax accounts may be preferable to many retirees. They don't have RMDs.

Chapter 12

RetireSmart—the Conclusion

The question isn't at what age I want to retire, it's at what income.

—George Foreman, former pro boxer and entrepreneur.

So here's my comprehensive data drive all-encompassing finale. Ready?

Step 1: save tax fees by using the standard deduction today.
Step 2: grow/withdraw tax free by using the capital-gain tax rate.
Step 3: pass on to heirs tax free by using the step-up in basis.

It's that simple.

If you need further proof, please continue reading. If not, go open a brokerage account and invest in a low-cost tax-managed sector fund.

Truer words have rarely been spoken (at least in terms of retirement planning), and they're particularly applicable to this conversation. How can you save and invest in a way that lets you reach your desired income level in retirement?

I approached that question in two ways in this book—negative and positive. So as I set you off to spread your wings and secure your own retirement, I'd like to leave you with two parting thoughts along those lines.

The negative—avoid 401(k) plans

As I'm sure you've gathered by now, I'm not a fan of 401(k) plans. I hope I've helped you understand why and have shown you a better way to achieve a financially secure retirement.

But I don't want to be too negative. There's a lot to like about 401(k) plans, as I've explained.

- They allow you to save up to $20,500 a year, pretax, with an additional $7,000 catch-up contribution allowed for those age fifty and older.
- Some employers match part of your contribution, giving you what amounts to free money. This is the number-one reason you would want to invest in a 401(k) plan.
- You can direct the manner in which your 401(k) funds are invested, and you may have a lot of choices, depending on what your plan offers—stocks, bonds, cash, or a combination of stocks and bonds and cash, depending on the level of risk you can tolerate.
- Earnings derived from investments in a 401(k) plan are not taxed; they're reinvested and compound over time.
- Finally, most 401(k) plans offer some level of flexibility if you're in a financial pinch. Depending on the circumstances, you can take a loan or a hardship withdrawal from your 401(k) plan. When you take a loan, you pay yourself back, meaning you collect the interest. That's better than a bank collecting the interest.

Even if all these "benefits" were appealing to you as a *gig* worker, a 401(k) isn't available to most of you.

The problem, at its most basic level, comes down to taxes.

I showed you an example of two people—Mr. Uninformed and Mrs. Smart—who invested the same money in a 401(k) account and an after-tax account and saw the money grow to the same amount at retirement.

Then Mr. Uninformed and Mrs. Smart retired and started a systematic withdrawal program, and that's where Mrs. Smart came out ahead because she understood that not all taxes are the same. If you have to be taxed, you want to be taxed at the long-term capital-gains tax rate. Mr. Uninformed wasn't; Mrs. Smart was.

Mrs. Smart also benefitted upon her death. While her death was surely a tragedy to all who loved her, her children received a step-up in cost basis to the value of the account at the date of death—a provision that doesn't apply to retirement accounts such as Mr. Uninformed. Now, Mr. Uninformed did have one benefit Mrs. Smart didn't—employer matches, as I mentioned a few paragraphs ago. And that's why I said that if you receive a match, investing in a 401(k) plan isn't quite such a bad idea. But you should invest only up to the level of the company match. In other words, if your company matches up to 4 percent, contribute 4 percent—not a penny more.

I hope that makes sense, and you were able to digest the rest of the book with an eye toward other options—specifically, the steps I set out in my introduction. They're shown below.

I'm not going to rehash those steps; you already read them. But I am going to revisit what is arguably the second-most important point I made: how you can beat the rigged tax system that makes 401(k) plans too problematic.

The positive—save your age divided by three

I think there's a much better way to save for retirement than 401(k) plans—after-tax accounts with a bit of discipline thrown in.

Of course, discipline is the hard part. Few of us want to make our beds, go to the gym, and load the dishwasher. Those things aren't fun. It's the same with saving for retirement.

But we desperately need to save for retirement. A stunning 21 percent of Americans have nothing at all saved for the future and another 10 percent have less than $5,000 tucked away, according to Northwestern Mutual's 2018 Planning and Progress Study.

"You know that retirement is coming," said Batya Shevich in *Warren Buffett: To Be Rich and Successful Is Easy!* "It isn't as though it just shows up one day and takes you by surprise, so you need to get ready for it."

So how do you find the discipline to save? I introduced my secret sauce for that discipline: take your age, divide it by three, and save that percentage of your gross salary.

Granted, this process ends up being a bit more complex than it sounds—at least if you don't start early. So let me explain it again in a slightly different way.

Say you're twenty-five and earn $50,000 a year. Your age (twenty-five) divided by three is 8.33 percent, and 8.33 percent of $50,000 is $4,165. So you'll need to save $4,165 per year to get on the path to secure retirement. That's just $347 per month. That's not bad, right?

Now let's say you wait to age thirty-five to start saving, and you (unfortunately) still earn $50,000 a year. We take your age (thirty-five) and divide it by three for 11.67 percent. Then we add that 11.67 percent to the original 8.33 percent (your penalty for not saving sooner) for a total savings rate of 20 percent. So starting at age thirty-five, you will need to save 20 percent of your $50,000 salary—$10,000 a year, $833 a month. Ouch! You may need to give up vacations, dining out, and cars that run reliably.

Now consider what would happen if you wait until age forty-five to start saving and still earn $50,000 a year. (Clearly, you should be looking for a job that offers annual inflation- or performance-based increases, but we'll ignore than for the purposes of this example.) Now you have to save your age (forty-five) divided by three, so 15 percent. And you would have to add to that 15 percent the 8.33 percent penalty for not starting to save at age twenty-five and the 11.67 percent penalty for not starting to save at age thirty-five, for a total savings rate of 35 percent. That would be $17,500 a year or $1,458 a month. You'll barely be able to pay your bills. In fact, you'll probably have to move in with your parents, or worse, your children.

It may sound tough, but remember what Dave Ramsey, the personal finance guru, once said, "Live like no one else, so later you can live and give like no one else."

All for you

To close, there's one final point I'd like to reiterate: none of this should discourage you from saving because you're convinced that you can't easily reach your goals.

Anything you can save today will make your life at least a little better tomorrow. And a little better counts for a lot.

I've advised many clients about money management over the years, and in the process, I've investigated every possible way to help people reach their retirement goals. And the first step to success has always been awareness. "Risk comes from not knowing what you're doing," said investing guru, Warren Buffett.

If you don't prepare, you'll end up in the same boat as many Americans, toiling away your golden years. According to the National Institute on Retirement Security, the gap between what Americans have saved and what they will need in retirement is estimated to be between $6.8 and $14 trillion. It's no surprise then that many are choosing to work at Walmart, Target, McDonald's, or other such establishments.

I hope, that with the help of this book, that won't be you.

So here are the three takeaways:

1. Standard deduction: The IRS does not tax the first $12,950 of earned income per person per year. Invest this into a tax-managed portfolio of no-load mutual funds that are suitable for your needs.
2. Capital gains deduction: The IRS does not tax the first $41,675 of long-term capital gains realized per person per year. You can withdraw this amount annually *tax free*. Can be combined with #1 (standard deduction) bringing the annual tax free total to $54,625!
3. Step up in basis: The IRS does not tax the first $12.06 million of assets passed to heirs. This can be used during life or at death. Pass your estate onto your loved ones *tax free*.

If you remember in the introduction, I asked you to imagine a retirement that offered the following benefits:

- Has no contribution limits
- Has no investment choice limitations
- Lets you touch your money when you need it most
- Knows the tax difference between income and capital gains
- Has no age restrictions on your money
- Has no distribution minimums
- Understands the tax code
- Has no 10 percent excise taxes on distributions
- Has no 1099Rs
- Has no administration expenses
- Can be funded from any source
- Has no CPA expenses
- Has no vesting requirements

Well, did I deliver on my promise? I think so. Remember, just follow my three takeaways and your personal tax-free gig retirement will be in your control.

RetireSmart! Amazon Customer Reviews

Amazon Customer
5.0 out of 5 stars. Practical retirement planning for the working-class American.

RetireSmart—the author demonstrated a keen understanding of the common workingman and woman then provided a road map to financial security for them to follow.

In my experience, most retirement strategic guides focus on the haves. In essence, "Retirement strategies and lower tax burdens are for the wealthy elite. If you're the average American, stop dreaming and get back to work." Refreshingly, this was not the case for *RetireSmart*.

The author invites debt-burdened Americans, the majority of Americans, to the table. At the table, he reassures them that retiring comfortably is possible for them just as well as the rich. Next, he outlines a program that systematically and painlessly leads that person out of debt and into the world of being able to invest in their future.

Grimaldi demystifies and simplifies complicated investment vehicles. As promised by the title, he shows how to navigate that world for the purpose of retiring with the highest possible retirement income and lowest tax burden. This information is helpful to both the haves and have-nots.

If you're a person who requires data to make informed decisions, the author describes multiple studies, statistical analysis, the evolution of tax code, government-sponsored retirement plans, the many acronyms for laws and investment modalities, along with the short- and long-term tax implications.

Personally, "*RetireSmart*, no taxes, no tolls, no fees, no traffic. Enjoy!" was enough terminology for me. I was hooked and wanted to read a step-by-step plan for achieving those goals. The book was written in such a way that the key points, the take-home messages were readily apparent—my needs were met. I plan to use *RetireSmart* investment strategies, as well as teach the information to my children.

Seasheils
5.0 out of 5 stars. RetireSmart!

Whahooo...finally! A book I can read when I don't have time and a book I can easily understand retirement, uncomplicated and logical. Thanks!

bigromster
5.0 out of 5 stars. Great information.

I received this as a gift a couple years prior to my retirement. Chock full of useful information and have passed it along to another soon-to-be retiree.

AR
5.0 out of 5 stars. Great guide!

Excellent book! The author takes a complex topic and simplifies it in such a way that the average reader/investor can easily follow and understand. His writing style is an easy yet direct approach to the topic geared for anyone regardless of status or wealth. This is an important topic that affects every workingman and woman. This book is a serious guide and should be on everyone's Christmas list!

MVA

5.0 out of 5 stars. A must-have book for retirement planning.

This is a must-have book for anyone starting a career, a must-have graduation gift! Mr. Grimaldi explains how to make it to retirement without losing your shirt in the process. His examples are clear (I'm not a numbers person!). His examples are easy to follow and his advice sound.

It's never too late to correct the course of retirement, this book will show you how.

David Ladyga

5.0 out of 5 stars. Great reading for beginning your retirement planning.

Reviewed in the United States on March 25, 2020

Mark goes into great detail with easy-to-understand examples of the tax perils of the hyped retirement options and how to get tax-*free* income.

Mark tells you what the wealthy do to protect their money, and it is not the same thing the everyday financial adviser tells you to do.

This is a must read for anyone thinking or planning to join their company's 401K plan to learn why they should or should not join.

Paul Stich

5.0 out of 5 stars. Guidelines for a safer, less daunting retirement.

Being ten years into retirement, Mark Grimaldi's new book hits home as a "coulda-woulda-shoulda" experience. In perspective, I did follow some of his suggestions but more by chance than by astute planning. There was a kind of unconscious karma that might have reflected his introductory "G-P-S" strategy, but it was not motivated by a grounded realization about the peril of taxation. *RetireSmart* provides just that.

The author's target audience are millennials and younger, and he provides them with wise strategies to incorporate into their immediate and long-range financial existence. He posits that each new generation has the possibility of living longer, which brings with it the need to anticipate a far different approach to long-range financial planning. Most in my generation merely coasted into retirement without a stratagem. Just the opening chapters hammer home the idea that neglecting focus on the "golden years" borders on sheer recklessness.

The author's powerful premise is that fewer and fewer of today's middle-class workers have the protection of pensions, and their unrelenting spending (including habitual refinancing of mortgages) places them in far greater economic peril in relation to their future. Prudence dictates a far greater clarity of purpose with regard to retirement.

That groundwork established, Grimaldi then arrives at his thesis: the grim assertion that the 401(k) plans, in their many forms, present a not-so-hidden but easily ignored dilemma. They provide a convenient remedy for retirement neglect and have been embraced by many employers, but they do not protect individuals from the pitfalls of post-employment taxation.

Susan F. Kollhoff
5.0 out of 5 stars. Important read.

This book lays out in simple steps how to retire tax free. Particularly enlightening is the history of the 401(k). Take a look. You won't be disappointed.

About the Author

Mark Anthony Grimaldi is a certified fund specialist, chief economist, money manager for the Sector Rotation Fund (NAVFX), noted economic forecaster, and multiple-award-winning author. He is known for his accurate economic forecasts and sector-rotation method of money management.

Portfolio management

In December 2009, Grimaldi became chief economist and money manager of the Sector Rotation fund, NAVFX. In this role, Grimaldi uses his thirty years of macroeconomic and investment-management experience to select the market sectors he believes have the most growth potential.

As of December 30, 2021, NAVFX has a five-star Morningstar Rating for the prior ten years. More recent performance can be obtained from Morningstar.com. The author doesn't guarantee the accuracy of any ranking services and knowledge that ranking can change at any time.

Media

Mr. Grimaldi has been interviewed on live television on several occasions. He also has done dozens of radio spots across the nation.

Teaching/college lectures

He coordinated and taught investment training classes on a college campus from 1989 to 2004. He also had in-depth lectures at SUNY Cobleskill in beautiful upstate New York.

Education

Grimaldi received a bachelor's degree in economics from Albany State University in 1985. He holds the Certified Fund Specialist (CFS) designation.

Economic Forecasting

During his career, Grimaldi forecasted a number of key economic events, including the following:

The 2007 housing-market correction. In March 2006, shortly before the S&P/Case-Shiller Home Price Index reached an all-time high of 188.93. Grimaldi wrote in his *Navigator* newsletter, "In the next five years, house values are going to return to their 1997 levels plus inflation." In the second quarter of 2009, the S&P/Case-Shiller Home Price Index reached a low of 111.11.

The 2008–2009 recession. In his December 2007 *Navigator* newsletter, Grimaldi wrote that "recession risk increased from 60 percent to 70 percent in 2008," and in his January 2008 newsletter, he wrote that "a recession begins in the middle of the year." Looking back, we now know that a recession formally began in December 2007 and lasted eighteen months until June 2009.

Skyrocketing unemployment. In January 2009, when the national unemployment rate was under 7 percent, Grimaldi wrote in his *Navigator* newsletter that unemployment would reach 10 percent nationally. On November 6, 2009, it did.

The 2010 "flash crash." In his January 2010 *Navigator* newsletter, Grimaldi called for "the first one thousand–point down day in the history of the Dow Jones Industrial Average in 2010." In the flash crash—the quick drop in stock prices that occurred on May 6, 2010—the Dow plunged approximately one thousand points.

The Money Compass

In 2014, Grimaldi coauthored *The Money Compass*, a plain-English guide to good investing that presents practical strategies and actionable advice for safely navigating today's financial markets (Wiley).

From the book's description:

> Between the ongoing recession, the collapse of the housing market, and the crumbling of the middle class, many Americans are left wondering what happened to the American dream. They're also wondering what happened to their money. For millions of people, just making ends meet is challenging enough. So when it comes to saving and investing, it seems like the deck is stacked against you. The bad news is that you're right. If the economy were a card game, the dealer would hold all the aces. But the good news is that you don't have to play by the house rules. Renowned for his unvarnished insight on finance and investing, money manager Mark Grimaldi has a reputation for telling it like it is. He doesn't sugarcoat the negative, and he doesn't have time for the financial industry hype that leads to bad investing decisions. Here's the truth: the economy is in bad shape, but that doesn't mean you can't save responsibly, invest profitably, and retire comfortably.
>
> In *The Money Compass*, Grimaldi teams up with accounting professor, G. Stevenson Smith, to offer a wealth of smart investing advice for today's investor. This plain-English guide to good

investing presents practical strategies and actionable advice for safely navigating today's financial markets. It shows you how to manage credit and debt responsibly, how to use the tax code to your advantage, which kinds of trendy investing advice you should ignore, and where to put your money for solid returns.

In addition, the authors explore the hard macroeconomic realities that explain how we got here and where we're going next. They look at the primary causes and consequences of the recession, the housing crash, the slow collapse of government programs, long-term unemployment, and how it all impacts you and your money. Plus, Grimaldi and Stevenson forecast the next big economic shock and show you how to profit from it.

The economic game is rigged to keep you poor and keep Wall Street rich. So it's time to write your own rules. Whether you're white collar, blue collar, or somewhere in between, *The Money Compass* gives you the commonsense guidance you need to chart a course to a comfortable financial future—even in the roughest economic waters.

Reviews of *The Money Compass* have been overwhelmingly positive.

I, like many Americans, have found myself sitting in the wasteland that once was my financial life. It seems nearly impossible to get ahead in these times. What am I doing wrong? How can I change this? These and many other questions I asked myself over the past five or six years. And then comes *The Money Compass*. Wow! Never have I read such a clear and concise synopsis on the economic world at large. Chapter after chapter provided not only new insights but confirmations of my past actions… Sure, I made poor choices, but then so did most folks. Rather than berating, the authors help us to understand how we *all* got here, who did it to us, and even give thoughts on how to avoid the same messes again.

Thanks, these words of wisdom, I feel better prepared to watch my financial back, protect what I have, and make better choices to get ahead in the future. Well written and an easy read, I'd recommend this to anyone who needs to regain their financial "bearing."

Probably the one thing that most people worry about is money. It seems you can never have too much but always there is too little. In *The Money Compass* by Mark Grimaldi and Stevenson Smith, you are given tools that help you take a proactive role in your own wealth.

This book is more than a preachy account of what you need to do, it is actually a good teacher in what you should do. There are many insightful exercises and tips on things you should do that you probably did not think about. The US has is slowly inching itself out of the great recession of 2008, and regardless of your situation, you should not be caught in the next one (which the author predicts is around the corner).

Money is only paper, and you need to take charge and steer the financial waters with a steady hand and the helpful book, *The Money Compass. The Money Compass* by Mark Grimaldi is an intellectual feast: referring back to the "America that once was." Mr. Grimaldi (the writer of the former "*Money Navigator Newsletter*," now the "*Money Compass*" newsletter) has a knack for explaining finance in a down-to-earth, easy-to-understand manner. I read the entire book in two sittings and urged my wife to read it as well. Mark is a conservative economist, so he explains the economy based on Wall Street and Washington. He discusses the "pickle" our country is in, from the "Federal Debt Bomb" to student loans to the lobbyists in DC. The subtitle: "Where Your Money Went and How to Get It Back" is an apt synopsis.

I am terribly afraid that America is on its way to becoming a "third world" country: Mr. Grimaldi with advice like "Live Below Your Means" and acquire "Academic Skills" is right on target. How in the world will we pay off $17 TRILLION of debt?

I would suggest you buy this book and keep a notepad nearby: you will surely benefit. Near the end, there are quotes of the economic forecasts the newsletter has made over the years. He predicts a 2014 recession… Hold on to your hat! (and your money): get this extraordinary book that is a "compass" to guide you through the world of finance.

Mark Grimaldi's *The Money Compass* points readers to sound waters. It begins with perspective on the erosion of national fiscal sanity and its consequences for both the society and the individual. It makes a clear case that traditional devices for preserving wealth have gone by the wayside in recent decades. While much of the survival advice is modest and workable for the average person, quite a bit is very high-powered and makes the case for engaging a financial advisor. The lesson is clear: having a compass in hand is useful, but it takes more than one hand to steer your vessel into safe harbors.

CPSIA information can be obtained
at www.ICGtesting.com
Printed in the USA
BVHW041309020522
635411BV00007B/12

9 781662 476143